RECONNECTING WITH NATURE: NEW HISTORIES

RETHINKING HUMAN–ANIMAL RELATIONSHIP

RECONNECTING WITH NATURE
NEW HISTORIES

JADAVPUR UNIVERSITY
HISTORY MONOGRAPH SERIES

Other titles in this series:

River, Society and Culture: Environmental Perspectives on the Rivers of Assam and Bengal
RUP KUMAR BARMAN

Indian Medicinal Plants in the Shifting Terrains of Science: Botanical and Medical Literature of Nineteenth-century Bengal
NUPUR DASGUPTA

The Gasping City: An Environmental History of Calcutta, 1817–1923
MAHUA SARKAR

RECONNECTING WITH NATURE: NEW HISTORIES

Rethinking Human–Animal Relationship

READING STORIES FROM BENGALI LITERATURE

Anuradha Roy

PRIMUS BOOKS

PRIMUS BOOKS
An imprint of Ratna Sagar P. Ltd.
Virat Bhavan
Mukherjee Nagar Commercial Complex
Delhi 110 009

Offices at CHENNAI LUCKNOW AGRA AHMEDABAD BENGALURU
BHOPAL COIMBATORE DEHRADUN GUWAHATI HYDERABAD JAIPUR
JALANDHAR KANPUR KOCHI KOLKATA MUMBAI PATNA RANCHI
VARANASI

First published 2023

ISBN: 978-93-5687-837-2 (Paperback)
ISBN: 978-93-5687-471-8 (POD)

Published by Primus Books

Laser typeset by Jojy Philip
jojyphilip@gmail.com

To

All dogs, from Maggie to Maniklal
and all cats, from Chika-Chika-Boom to Ini-Mini
as well as a few members of other non-human species
who helped make my life rich and meaningful

Contents

Foreword

The research programme on environmental history of South Asia was initiated in the Department of History, Jadavpur University, under the University Grants Commission's Special Assistance Programme (SAP) in 2004. I had the privilege to head the programme during its first two phases. This programme was the first of its kind in the country. This centre for environmental history gradually earned recognition both within the country and beyond. The faculty members of the department have already published quite an impressive number of books and articles on the subject. Such publications grew out of the several SAP-funded research projects undertaken at our centre. A large number of international and national conferences, on various themes of environmental history, were organized and the department also hosted about twenty outstanding scholars in the field as visiting professors. I have already mentioned in my edited volumes *Situating Environmental History* (2007, new edn., 2021) and *Critical Themes in Environmental History of India* (2020) and in my recent monograph, *Climate, Calamity and the Wild* (Primus Books, 2022) that though environmental history is one of the most important areas of enquiry in the field of history, it still remains as a less explored field without well-defined disciplinary standards and methodological strategies. It is felt that professional historians with the requisite methodological training will be able to (a) develop and define the agenda and disciplinary canons of this field of inquiry, and (b) historicize the present-day concerns and anxieties in the broad area of environmental history.

In his recent book *The Climate of History in a Planetary Age* (Primus Books, 2021), Dipesh Chakrabarty argues that historians need to revise many of their fundamental assumptions and methodologies in this period of human-induced climate change. While confronting environmental issues today, when globalization has triggered the threat of global warming and mass extinction, historians are inventing new conceptual categories to integrate questions that they have usually treated in the past as separate and virtually unconnected. This finds manifestation in the recent rise of the term 'environmental humanities'. It is an interdisciplinary umbrella category that accommodates environmental history, environmental philosophy, cultural geography, ecocriticism, cultural anthropology, political and social ecology and so on. Humans have been engaged in a meaningful intellectual dialogue with the earth as a category since the post-Second World War period, but the planet as a category was not visible earlier. Now, under the threat of global warming, humans have come face to face with planetary categories as well, aided by post-humanist scholars like Bruno Latour. This marks the beginning of a communicative relationship between humans and the planet. Now the way has been paved for the emergence of the planet as a historical category. The formalized emergence of planetary humanities as another useful conceptual category is just a matter of time. Historians need to connect deep and recorded histories and establish conversational links between the historical time and geological and biological times. This will enable the historians to tell the larger story of how a particular biological species, Homo sapiens, along with its Technosphere, as well as other species that co-evolved with or were dependent on them, came to dominate the entire planet within a short span of time.

The human–nature interface has been the most fundamental issues in whatever decisions human society has taken since time immemorial. One of the aspects of the inner conflicts within human societies of the past was fuelled by the continuous effort to resolve the question relating to the legitimate use of the natural world. As human settlements spread across the earth and as technology advanced, the urge to resolve this fundamental question intensified. An overarching denial of this issue by humankind, armed with the Technosphere, especially in recent decades, has completely disrupted the natural balance of the planet. It is now the final call for historians to address and resolve this fundamental question. The connection between the legitimate use of natural world and its connection with power and profit has put environmental issues on an equal footing with historical categories like race, class, gender, ethnicity, and nationalism. However, even in the face of a growing environmental crisis, humanity has shown a kind of indifference to environmental issues while giving more emphasis to power and politics. The present series, like many others in recent years, urge historians to reorient minds to the need of the hour, i.e. concern for Planet Earth.

The present series 'Reconnecting with the Nature' contains four different monographs: Rup Kumar Barman's *River, Society and Culture: Environmental Perspectives on the Rivers of Assam and Bengal*; Nupur Dasgupta's *Indian Medicinal Plants in the Shifting Terrains of Science: Botanical and Medical Literature of Nineteenth-century Bengal*; Anuradha Roy's *Rethinking Human–Animal Relationship: Reading Stories from Bengali Literature*; and Mahua Sarkar's *The Gasping City: An Environmental History of Calcutta, 1817–1923* is the outcome of a commendable effort towards re-establishing the human–nature interface.

River, Society and Culture: Environmental Perspectives on the Rivers of Assam and Bengal critically analyses the migration crisis and river–human relationships. The discourse offers an understanding of the lesser-explored society and culture of the Titash-Tista-Kalahi-Raidak basins of Bengal, Assam, and Bhutan from an environmental perspective. *Indian Medicinal Plants in the Shifting Terrains of Science: Botanical and Medical Literature of Nineteenth-century Bengal* traces the processes of medical and botanical reconnaissance during the nineteenth century, with a focus on indigenous medicinal plants, and also observes their integration into the framework of modern science. In *Rethinking Human–Animal Relationship: Reading Stories from Bengali Literature*, the author argues that animal studies should be considered a growing interdisciplinary field. The historiography of this field shows a 'moral schizophrenia' of human beings towards animal 'others'. It further seeks to connect the unrelenting exploitation of animals throughout history to the domination of humans by humans—oppression of women, racial and community struggles, etc. Finally, *The Gasping City: An Environmental History of Calcutta, 1817–1923* begins with an explanation of the intricate relationship between the development of cityscapes and its impact on the surrounding environment. Set between the period of 1817 and 1923, it also analyses the responses and attitudes of the educated urban people to ongoing environmental changes. Whether the traits of a 'planned city' was compatible or incompatible with the sustainable growth of environment is the main thrust area of this monograph.

With the publication of the present series—'Reconnecting with Nature'—I have no doubt that the immense potentials and possibilities of environmental history will be further refurbished. The grand quest to reach a resolution pertaining to the legitimate use of nature, I believe, will continue to dominate the discipline of history and its related knowledge systems. Environmental histories and environmental humanities will continue to thrive because the seeds of a new social and cultural history are firmly embedded in it. The importance of the present series has to be understood in this broader context.

RANJAN CHAKRABARTI

Note on the Series

Could history have been made without nature as the nurturing site for living species, without the primordial bounty of water, flora, and fauna? How did the hominids create their own space in this, the rarest of planets in the known orbit of the universe? How well have we been able to attain and preserve this? Can we sustain this with the progression of 'civilization' as we understand it? These are fundamental matters in environmental studies today and the questions take us beyond the rigidly defined contours of the discipline of history, which was specifically built around the human species. History is now observed to include much wider frames and perspectives.

The Department of History, Jadavpur University, is the first academic institution in the country to begin running a UGC-sponsored DRS Project on the History of Environment, with Professor Ranjan Chakravarti as the coordinator, from 2005. He successfully built the foundations of the discipline in the department. Within a decade, the programme achieved the level of a UGC DSA-I Special Assistance Project in 2015. The project has then been steered successively by Professor Amit Bhattacharya and Professor Mahua Sarkar. I was put in charge in 2018 and have supervised the programme till its completion in 2020. The department has witnessed a long tradition of research in the history of environment and allied subjects. The last few years from 2018 to 2020 saw a fresh bout of research by the faculty. The proposal for the publication of a few such research works was approved by the authorities of Jadavpur University in 2019–20. The outcome is showcased in the present series of books. The series consists of four short monographs, each devoted to a different theme, embodying distinct areas of research under the overarching theme of environmental history. Thematically, some major and new areas of concern have been addressed in each work. The authors focus on elemental nature and human life around it. Thus, rivers, flora, fauna, and ecology in the urban context have been chosen as the major sites of investigation; the discussions here are distinctly designed to present new perspectives. An inkling of the overall philosophy of research has been briefly projected above. The authors, in their various contexts and approaches, project the deeper urge of the historian to illuminate the profundity of the existence of life on the Blue Planet. This short note on the series does not intend to delve any deeper into the themes and the underlying concerns they present. These have been well illuminated in the authors' respective introductions to their books.

I end this note by extending my thanks to those without whose support we could not have run the programme nor would this series have seen the light of day. First and foremost, I am beholden to the Hon'ble Vice-Chancellor of Jadavpur University, Professor Suranjan Das, for constant academic inspiration and advice. My sincerest thanks go to him and the authorities of the university for providing all the facilities required for carrying out the long-term project in the Department of History. I must express my deepest gratitude to all my colleagues in the department and outside it for their unstinted support. I am indebted to Professor Ranjan Chakrabarti, Professor Amit Bhattacharya, and Professor Mahua Sarkar, who were extremely generous in offering help and advice in running the programme and in carrying out the task of publications. Professor Anuradha Roy and Professor Rup Kumar Barman have been ready with all suggestions and help about the publication process. Sri Hemendranath Mandal, Sri Bholanath Mandal, and Sri Ritwik Bagchi, the research assistants associated with the programme, deserve high praise for helping me to carry out my duties throughout these years. The office staff, the librarians, and the library staff of the department have been extremely helpful and diligent in providing all support. I am ever so grateful for that. Finally, we owe much to our publishers, Primus Books, for ready support and for keeping us on schedule. I especially thank Mr B.N. Varma for showing interest in the project. Dr Prasun Chatterjee has extended great support through the process of publication, without which our project might have languished. I would like to extend profuse thanks to Ms Jyotika Mansata for taking the utmost care in preparing the manuscripts. Finally, I acknowledge with the deepest gratitude our indebtedness to the University Grants Commission for making it possible for the whole project and this series to come to fruition.

NUPUR DASGUPTA

Acknowledgements

This book is an outcome of my love and concern for animals. I must express gratitude to my family, who kindled this love and shared my concerns. It has been wonderful growing up taking care of animals assisted by family members—not only pets at home, but also stray animals like an injured dog, a wounded pigeon, and a cow in labour, to mention a few. Love was combined with a serious intellectual quest regarding human–animal relationships when, a few years ago, I undertook a research project on the subject, under the UGC-sponsored DSA programme for the Department of History, Jadavpur University. I gratefully remember the encouragement received from my departmental colleagues, some of whom also share my passion for animals. I would like to make special mention of Professor Nupur Dasgupta, who was in charge of the programme when I finally wrote this book and who constantly encouraged me not only because it was her duty, but because we are on the same wavelength as far as our attitude towards animals are concerned. I am also grateful to Dr Mrinmoyee Deb, who teaches at the Government College of Art and Craft, Kolkata, for digging out suitable images for the cover.

ANURADHA ROY

Prologue

Animal studies is a growing academic field that is yet to have much of an impact in India. It is pursued in order to gain a better understanding of human beings' relationship with non-humans as well as to gain clarity regarding how to better that relationship. I thought of engaging with animal studies with both these aims. I know this is a daunting task, as animal studies is an interdisciplinary field involving a number of disciplines of both science and humanities and I cannot claim any expertise in most of them. My own discipline, history, has had some interaction with animal studies for some time, but those remain mostly outside the purview of the history we usually teach or research. So far as the aim of improving the relationship is concerned, *Homo sapiens*, from the very beginning of their history, have sought to dominate other species. Our lifestyle and thoughts had been shaped by our culture's human/animal binary and our utilitarian and aggressive attitude to animals well before we came to reflect about it. Therefore, one cannot really hope to change things by writing a book. But I hope this effort of mine, will become a small contribution to animal studies with special reference to India (specifically Bengal), will help the readers rethink human–animal relationship.

In everyday life, human–animal relationships are generally of a gross and crude nature. Humans have a biased and arbitrary understanding of what animals mean and, furthermore, they have multiple and paradoxical meanings for us—as good or bad omens, religious icons, subjects of personal affection, part of the work force, food, etc. Whether or not they deserve moral treatment from us often depends on whether they are cute or ugly, pets or wild, edible or non-edible. Yet, there is a general human amorality regarding animals. Even if some of us care for animals this does not produce a general love for them. Thus, we can have our animals and eat them too. This attitude is based on an ontological simplification, which is borne out by the very term 'animal', a non-generic word that homogenizes radically different forms of life and makes us think of them in reductionist and essentialist terms. In our view, there is a great divide: we stand alone on one side and all other beings are on the other side. The latter are considered the 'absolute others'[1] and inevitably inferior to us. Thus, we believe we can use them, abuse them and even kill them mercilessly. If an animal is killed, it is not considered murder.

Increasing industrialization and urbanization in modern times have further widened the distance between humans and animals, although emotional investment in pets seeks to compensate for this loss. We also value some 'charismatic megafauna' like tigers, lions and rhinos and try to facilitate their survival, which, we think, would somewhat temper our propensity towards consumer capitalism. However, such thinking provides further impetus to commodification of animals by encouraging theme parks, and such other artificial habitations. Equally purposefully, animals as religious icons like the cow draw our reverence, but other animals remain mere objects or natural resources to be consumed or exploited in other ways. Morality has never dominated human attitude to the animal world, nor has compassion. Our attitude to animals is motivated by many considerations—religious, ecological, scientific, cultural, academic, and above all, utilitarian. Only in some individual cases it becomes attachment and love, which applies mostly to our pets.

I am part of this culture too. Apparently, I have loved animals from my childhood and taken care of many of them. They are mostly dogs and cats, rabbits and guinea pigs, and on rare occasions, cows and pigeons. But I have got many fishes and chickens killed to feed dogs and cats. I consume fish and chicken myself (though I find the fish and meat corner in the market an abominable sight and avoid it). I have eaten pork and other meats too, though mostly abroad, due to their unavailability nearer home. I used to eat mutton as well, and regularly too, for a long time; but then an encounter with a scene of goat sacrifice during Durga Puja, made me give it up. Still, I have to admit, my compassion for animals does not extend to vegetarianism. Like many people, I don't like to give much thought to the animals I eat. I eat meat, not animals. This is a self-deceit common to humans. We tend to objectify the animals with whom we have only a utilitarian relationship.

I write this book mainly to face my own self-deceit, which one may even call hypocrisy. But not only me, humankind in its entirety seems to nurture considerable complexities, confusions and contradictions as far as animals are concerned, which I would like to address through this volume. Let me emphasize: this is an attempt to *address* the problem, knowing full well that *redressal* is beyond one's capabilities.

In this book I engage with animal studies without making much original contribution, in the sense that not much primary material has been used in this effort. It is perhaps 're-search' in a spiritual sense, but not much of research, speaking strictly academically. Yet, modern Bengali literature has a wealth of stories to offer on human–animal relationships, which I had read for sheer pleasure in the past. After delving into animal studies in the first chapter of this book, I will then turn to these stories in the second chapter to read them once again, now with a more analytical approach, and see how they corroborate the insights gleaned from animal studies, take those insights into more depth and even go beyond them. The writers of these tales tried to rethink human–animal relationships with deep care and concern for both and, removing the human cultural blinders, they have tried to take our relationship with animals beyond our usual speciesism. They urge the readers to do some rethinking about the matter. Not me, but these writers can thus claim to have made some original contributions to animal studies. For me, this chapter is an attempt to combine my love for animals with my love for literature.

* * *

I wrote the final version of this monograph during the forced leave from my regular classes and other university duties due to the lockdown necessitated by the Covid-19 pandemic, which made this exercise seem more meaningful. First, the source of this pandemic was clearly thoughtless human savagery towards animals, and second, the scare that it created—the fear of death and a desperate urge to live—brought us very close to our fellow non-human creatures. Let me explain.

Scientists tend to agree that the Coronavirus was transferred from a bat to a human, probably through a pangolin, and that it happened in the wet markets of Wuhan, China. Though this is often blamed on the Chinese culture of eating wild animals, we perhaps need to further consider this matter. Zoonotic transfer of diseases is becoming increasingly more common, not only in China, but everywhere: HIV, Ebola of West Africa, Zika virus of Brazil, Nipah virus of Malaysia and MERS of Middle East are some recent examples which emerged from other parts of the world. In fact, such transfer has been a major menace since the early modern period, when the correlated processes of capitalism, urbanization, industrialization and colonization increased the insensitive human use of animals manifold. Demand for meat increased in cities, leading to an increase in the number of livestock raised artificially. The horror of the Smithfield Market of London described in *Oliver Twist* readily comes to mind. Animals satisfied not only human hunger, but also human ego. From the 1840s, menageries were set up in London to exhibit exotic animals from the distant colonies, thereby boosting imperialist pride. Sometimes dinners were organized where such animals were special items on the menu. One such dinner in 1863 served bird's nest soup, kangaroo ham, Syrian pig, Chinese sheep, etc.[2] This unprecedented aggression towards animals often endangered human existence as well. Historians have recounted many instances of animals, being taken by Europeans to the colonies, devastating the lives of native animals and humans who had never had a chance to develop immunity against the diseases carried by these transported animals.[3]

The process of zoonotic transfer intensified from the 1990s, as capitalism took a new and extreme form in its neoliberal avatar. China, with its communist experiments being over and done, decided to follow this neo-capitalist path and it is well known that fresh initiates are always more enthusiastic about an ideology. Wuhan, China's industrial hub, symbolizes the spirit of the neoliberal, globalized, consumerist capitalism in many ways. Behind its spectacular gloss lies painful poverty and various lung diseases that affect a large section of the population. Its wet markets have thrived not so much to cater to the ordinary Chinese but to a handful of rich, who have been amassing more and more wealth every day and who find the consumption of wild animals very fulfilling. These animals are also exploited and exported for perceived 'medicinal cures'. This semi-legal trade in wild animals has been destroying their natural habitat and bringing them closer to humans, increasing zoonotic transfer.[4]

The result is the proliferation of diseases like Covid-19, which turned the upper and middle-class utopia all over the world into a dystopia. The pandemic caused many people to wake up to the plight of the hitherto-invisible *precariat* left in the lurch during the lockdown in a power-crazy and greedy social order. Even I, who had been mentioning the precariat for quite some years while teaching labour history (though we teach mostly about the proletariat, that is, workers of different organized sectors—the precariat is yet to find a place in the discipline of history), found this a true 'real'-ization! Alongside this, the systematic abuse of another largely invisible category was detected too. One now realizes more clearly how animals have been tortured and killed with impunity by humans throughout history, but increasingly and more terribly during modern times. The exploitation of humans by humans and of animals by humans indeed appear to be two interrelated historical processes.

With death staring us in the face and an urge to live leading to a suspension of much of our superfluous cultural activities, forcing us to put our fetishism on hold and look for minimum creature comforts, one had to seriously reflect on mankind's impact on nature, thanks to the pandemic. We came to the realization that howsoever rich and powerful one may be, nature would nevertheless treat him/her equally with all other hapless creatures sacrificed at the altar of civilization so far, including both humans and non-humans. The importance of nature came to the fore during the lockdown. One also realized the simple truth that humans and non-humans belong to the same nature or animal world, the biosphere if you will, and that the fear of death and urge to live is something very basic to the world of living that all creatures share. At the same time, however, one also realized the simple joy of living, just living! During the pandemic, one got to see numerous videos showing how, with culture beating a retreat, nature gloriously revealed herself everywhere like an epiphany: kangaroos were hopping around the streets of Adelaide, sea lions basked in the sunshine in Mar Del Plata, Argentina, and flamingos enjoyed themselves in Palm Beach, Mumbai. After a long time, a variety of birds were visiting our gardens and chirping to their hearts' content, blooming flowers were looking especially bright and a beautiful rainbow could be seen in the sky from the verandah of our locked-down houses after a short spell of shower.[5] Such rare experiences made me realize the deeper meaning of Rabindranath Tagore's poem 'Praner Ras' (The Essence of Life): 'The birds are singing with all the treasure stored in their voice / Theirs is a silent history, which says only this much—'We are, We live,/We live in this wonderful moment'![6] It also reminded me of Jibanananda Das' craving for 'the life of the magpie and the grasshopper'.[7] Indeed, it seems non-humans live more intensely than humans, because they are happy in their mere being. This understanding had been aptly summarized by Frankfurt school scholars Theodor W. Adorno and Max Horkheimer: 'To achieve the condition of an animal at the level of reflection—that is freedom', and of course, peace.[8] The pandemic made one realize that we humans should perhaps learn the meaning of living from the non-humans, and discarding all our vanity and selfishness, should live for all living beings—not only humans, but also non-humans. Poets and thinkers have often told us this before. But we have mostly thought of it as a cliché. In this 'age of epidemics', being in a tight spot, at least some of us feel it would be worth seriously reflecting on this.

Will the post-Corona world be a better place for all humans and animals? Or shall we go back to our normal civilized order, which was, in fact, most abnormal? Only the future will tell.

Notes

1. Jacque Derrida, *The Animal Therefore I Am*, tr. David Wills, New York: Fordham University Press, 2008.

2. Brian Fagan, *The Intimate Bond: How Animals Shaped Human History*, New York and London: Bloomsbury, 2015.

3. Alfred W. Crosby, *Ecological Imperialism: The Biological Expansion of Europe, 900–1900*, New York: Cambridge University Press, 1986.

4. Anindita Nag, 'Wuhan To Amaderi Kirti', *Anandabazar Patrika*, 22 April 2020.

5. Though I feel somewhat ashamed while writing this. It cannot but bring to my mind what the Italian author Francesca Melandri wrote during the crisis ('Letter to the French from the Future', *Liberation*, 28 March 2020) – 'Class will make all the difference. Being locked up in a house with a pretty garden is not the same as living in an overcrowded housing project. Nor is being able to work from home or seeing your job disappear.' And, even the animal world was facing trouble in various ways during the crisis. In Lopburi in Thailand monkeys no longer fed by tourists were fighting in the streets. If nature is beautiful, it also means a fierce struggle for survival.

6. Rabindranath Tagore, 'Praner Ras', *Shyamali*, 1343 BS/1936; included in *Rabindra Rachanabali*, vol. 20, Kolkata: Visva-Bharati, 1967.

7. Jibanananda Das, 'Aat Bachar Ager Ekdin', *Jibananda Das-er Shreshtha Kabita*, Kolkata: Bharvi Publication, 1954.

8. Max Horkheimer and Theodor W. Adorno, *Dialectic of Enlightenment: Philosophical Fragments*, 1947; repr. in English, New York: Continuum International Publishing Group, 1969.

1

Engaging with Animal Studies

Deep Unreason and Moral Schizophrenia Regarding the Animal 'Others'

Theodor W. Adorno and Max Horkheimer of the Frankfurt school, while addressing the civilizational questions raised by Karl Marx and trying to interpolate and expand Marxian thought, were inevitably drawn to the animal question.[1] They sought to theorize and problematize society's troubling relationship with animals long before the present trend of animal studies began, when it was quite uncharacteristic of the intellectual climate. They showed how the Aristotelian 'rational man' seems most irrational as far as his relationship with animals was concerned, unless it was considered as mere 'instrumental reason'. In Horkheimer's view, the skyscraper of a society is based on the suffering of many hierarchical stratums, the lowest of which is constituted by animals. The stratums are thus arranged: the monopoly capitalists at the top, then the petite bourgeoisie and landowners, service workers, bureaucrats, skilled industrial workers, the unskilled, the unemployed, the colonized people, and even below them the animals. The basement of this theoretical skyscraper is a slaughterhouse while the roof is cathedral, 'but from the windows of the upper floors, it affords a really beautiful view of the starry heaven'.[2] In this way, write Horkheimer and Adorno, 'Unreasoning creatures have encountered reason throughout the ages—in war and peace, in arena and slaughterhouse....'[3] They critiqued Western thought (German idealism and Judeo-Christian thought in particular) for their instrumentalist attitude towards animals, regarding it as part of the human instrumental attitude towards nature and referring to it as a manifestation of sadism. They called into question human dishonesty regarding this matter. Indeed, we usually do not allow animals to enter and upset our system of ethics. Human attitude toward animals is also viewed as a manifestation of 'moral schizophrenia' by a number of animal studies scholars nowadays, who simply find it indefensible.[4] Anticipating the latter, Horkheimer and Adorno also linked the 'unrelenting exploitation' of animals to the domination of humans by humans—for example, the oppression of women, racial minorities, workers and the like—through parallel and related social processes.

Indeed, human cruelty to animals is practically indescribable. Maybe there are people who like animals, or at least some of them, at the individual level, but on the whole animals are considered mere food or unpaid labour. Violence is perpetrated on animals not just for food and other necessities, they are also tortured for sheer entertainment, something that humans practice on members of their own species as well. For animals, however, humans tend to excuse this behaviour by stating that animals are like automatons and have no feeling, which shows their insensitivity and (deliberate) ignorance. Human beings are conveniently forgetful of the fact that animals are living creatures just like them and that they are sentient beings. This is associated with human essentialism and an anthropocentric view of the world, which in its turn has largely emerged from a nature–culture split. Of course, attempts have been made throughout human history to interrogate this split and close the gap between humans and animals, but the need for such initiatives seem to be getting more and more urgent these days. We are being urged to realize that the world does not revolve around humans, to discard human essentialism and to question the hyper-separated boundaries between the sacred human and the profane natural.

Nature does not differentiate between humans and animals. As such, we are not external to nature, howsoever important our culture seems to us and howsoever distant we feel from nature due to this. Our relationship with animals is not always culturally generated For example, when animals like crocodiles and tigers treat humans as meaty prey and this was quite common in a not so distant past which is evident from the Bengali saying 'jole kumir dangay bagh', i.e. 'the crocodile in water and the tiger on land').On the other hand, animals too have a form of culture; some, like apes have even been observed to make tools. We humans have only taken culture to a greater height— whether for better or for worse, we cannot really say. We must also realize that humans are a form of animal too, that we have evolved from the apes and, if we take a longer evolutionary view, from even simpler organisms. This was a process of not only biological evolution, but what is being called biology-culture co-evolution today. Nature and culture may still be valid historical categories, but no longer do they represent the strict animal-human boundary. We are very much alike. As Brett Walker, a scholar of animal studies, says, 'Look around carefully; look at your fingernails, hair and incisors: we were not built in the likeness of gods, but in the likeness of the other organisms with whom we share the earth'.[5] Thus, it is clear that the anthropocentric view of the world has been powerfully challenged recently.

Furthermore, we must realize that even though our cognitive brain is much bigger than that of any non-human animal, as far as feelings are concerned, animals, particularly those with composite brains similar to ours (as is the case with higher mammals), have complex and layered feelings, as the science of feeling has clearly shown. Emergence of feelings took place during the process of evolution with the development of the nervous system (which all vertebrates have, and some non-vertebrates as well). Even simpler creatures, as well as plants, sense and respond to stimuli in their environments, and all of them fight to maintain their physical wellbeing. This feeling gradually became more and more 'conscious' in the process of evolution. It is only our extreme human exceptionalism that has denied feelings to animals. Neuroscientists today have shown that even humans are driven more by feelings than their cognitive brain and that feelings play a fundamental role in our culture.[6] These feelings, which give us subjecthood and agency, give the same qualities to animals as well. Therefore, our kinship and resemblance to them is overwhelming, and realizing this is important to the process of understanding ourselves—how we came to be and who we are.

Ruling Animals Like a 'Banana Republic' Dictator: A Look into History

In recent times, Yuval Noah Harari has provided a deep and broad view of history, paying particular attention to human–animal relationships. He also treats humans as animals—the most oppressive and destructive among all of them.[7] Humans—to be precise, the species called *Homo sapiens*—were insignificant, like many other animals such as gorillas or jellyfish, when they first appeared in East Africa about 300,000 years ago. However, *Homo sapiens* then were the most cognitively developed of all animals. As a result of this 'cognitive revolution' they developed unique ways of thinking and communicating. This enabled them to destroy not only their brethren Hominid species, the Neanderthals, but gradually, as they migrated out of Africa to all over the world, innumerable animal species as well. Giant animals particularly suffered at the hands of humans, resulting in ecological disasters. Humans quickly became the top predator and jumped to the top of the food chain from a middle position. Harari shows that this spectacular leap had enormous consequences. Other animals at the top of the food chain, such as lions and sharks, had evolved into that position gradually, over millions of years. This enabled the ecosystem to develop checks and balances that prevented such predators from wreaking havoc on natural ecosystems. For example, as lions became deadlier, gazelles evolved to run faster. In contrast, humankind, with its huge cognitive capacity, ascended to the top of the food chain so quickly that the ecosystem was not given time to adjust. Other top predators were majestic creatures full of self-confidence. *Homo sapiens*, by contrast, were, in the words of Harari, 'more like a banana republic dictator'. Full of fears and anxieties about their position, they proved to be doubly cruel and dangerous. They began considering themselves as the epitome of creation, and a big chasm developed between them and the rest of the animal kingdom. What followed was a story of terrible violence and genocide. Tolerance is not a trademark of *Homo sapiens*. Human civilization has thus left a long trail of animal victims.

The 'cognitive revolution' marked the beginning of insulation between humans and nature. Since then:

Sapiens have been living in a dual reality. On the one hand, there is the objective reality of rivers, trees, lions; and on the other hand, the imagined reality of gods, nations, corporations. As time went by, the imagined reality became more powerful, so today the very survival of rivers, trees and lions depends on the grace of imagined entities like United States and Google.[8]

This is a big difference between human and nonhuman animals. The former nurture the illusion that they are the kings of all they survey. Animals are more down to earth, more realistic. Also, they have more control over their bodies and senses, as otherwise they would not have survived. Good observation, agility, physical dexterity and similar qualities are must for them.

Harari writes the history of Homo sapiens through three 'revolutions'. Following the cognitive revolution were the agricultural and industrial revolutions. During the agricultural revolution, *Homo sapiens* started domesticating animals. These were livestock used for work, meat, wool, etc., though the dog helping humans in hunting and fighting was the first animal domesticated and this had happened before the agricultural revolution. The spread of farming brought about the second wave of extinction of animals, and with the third wave following industrial activities there began intense exploitation of animals. Colonization in the modern period has also devastated ecosystems and wiped out many native species.[9] Even many of the animal species that survived (farm animals, pack animals, laboratory animals etc.) did so by being tailored to human needs and suffering terribly in the process.

It is argued that for a long time—well into the medieval period—humans felt a close kinship with animals.[10] The paleolithic hunter regarded his prey as a powerful ritual partner and looked upon the latter with respect. It has been said about the totem worship of early humans, 'We must be careful not to consider totemism a sort of animal worship.... Their [humans and their totems] relations are rather those of two things who are on the same level and of equal value.'[11] Even after animals were domesticated, a close relationship existed between the herders and the herded. The animals were not just food or slaves, but part of their daily life. With the further progress of civilization and urbanization, their utility increased, and yet the intimate relationship between animals and people was not uncommon, which was ultimately a relationship between two individuals. Historians are yet to write a history of human–animal relationships in the context of India, but from what we know about Europe—England in particular—it is evident that farmers in the Middle Ages shared their houses with their livestock. These were often long houses that were a combination of dwellings and animal byres. Herds were small, and shepherds knew each animal individually including their faces and footprints. Cattle received names and thus a kind of genuine partnership existed.

Farmers began moving animals out of their homes during the seventeenth and eighteenth centuries, though such cohabitation persisted in some places into the nineteenth and the twentieth centuries. However, with the steady growth of urban populations and with the onset of the Industrial Revolution, these intimate ties gave way to an intensified dichotomy between pride of ownership on the one hand and the animal as a mere commodity on the other. Things were drastically changing particularly in cities, also in much of the countryside. By the eighteenth century, controlled breeding of farm animals reached a new level as cities created an insatiable demand for meat, turning animals into sources of meat and turning the meat into money. More and more animals were forced into labour in different sectors and cruelty to them was considered normal. In cities and towns the situation was terrible: animals were crowded into houses and small yards and often roamed the streets as public nuisance. In villages, herds became larger with an increasing number of fattened beasts for sale. Animals were depersonalized and became mere statistics based purely on their marketability. Cruelty and savagery to animals became too glaring. Even man's good old co-species like dogs and horses received brutal treatment, despite the fact that images of cavalry charging into battle evoked powerful emotions of heroic nationalism and despite the fact that keeping dogs and cats as pets became more and more popular from about this time.

The rising enthusiasm for pets—dogs and cats in particular—in eighteenth-century England surely looks paradoxical in this context. Pets were not commodities or tools but companions, even members of the family. They were individuals with personalities. Perhaps this individualization of animals came with individuation of humans themselves, which is a hallmark of modernity. This questioned the dominant Christian belief that animals lacked the capacity to feel. Memorializing pets with epitaphs and poems became commonplace. However, this love for pets was associated with gender and class bias. Certain animal companions to women came to occupy a distinct leisurely role and denoted upper-class status. This is revealed by the popularity of ladies' lapdogs (spaniels, pugs), which, by boosting the patriarchal cult of domesticity, contributed to a domestic space idealized as the refuge for men from work—primarily women and children, but also pets. This was also supposed to help the upper classes maintain a civilized identity vis-à-vis both colonized populations and the lower classes at the imperial centre, though gradually the urge for pet-keeping reached the middle and lower levels of society as well. While pets became a virtual obsession for the upper-class people, and while pet cats and dogs were anthropomorphized, romanticized and pampered, stray animals or those kept by the working classes were considered a threat and treated without mercy. Moreover, as Harriet Ritvo shows in his book *The Animal Estate*, the Victorians used animal breeding to resolve class anxieties. As industrialization strained the English class structure, breeders of horses and dogs created elaborate class systems, replete with blue books and pedigrees patterned after those of the nobility.[12]

The rapidly changing nineteenth-century world encouraged compensatory attachment to pets. Concern for animals sometimes encompassed those who could have been pets, e.g. street mongrels, carters' dogs, etc., but other animal lives mostly remained devalued. By sentimentalizing pets people tended to hide animals and their sufferings in general from public view and hence from public responsibility. But, of course, pet-keeping implicitly argued for the worth of animal life.[13] It at least enabled the notion that animals had characters and personalities, which entitled them to moral treatment.

Another factor regarding the treatment of animals concerned significant changes in the discursive field. Indeed, in the post-Enlightenment period, there developed an empathy concerning animals. In 1824 the Society for Prevention of Cruelty to Animals was established in England (which, in 1840, became the Royal SPCA). Laws were enacted to protect animals against mistreatment, but these were not very effective and betrayed a great deal of ambivalence. For example, an 1835 legislation was aimed firmly at lower-class blood sports, animal baiting and animal fighting, while gentlemen's sports such as fishing, fox hunting and shooting continued to flourish. Meanwhile, animal vivisection had become widespread to serve modern science, and a concern for live vivisection developed at the same time. However, the scientists' utilitarian justification for this practice and the evocation of human good stood in the way of compassion and arguments were made for regulated and humane vivisection, though, of course, there were arguments to exempt dogs and cats from vivisection. Thus, whatever pro-animal attitude developed in these times represented only selective benevolence.[14] Many of the measures taken in eighteenth- and nineteenth-century England did not show genuine concern for animals. These were, at most, 'welfarist' measures seeking to regulate animal exploitation rather than prevent it.[15] More often than not, they emerged out of human self-interest. For example, the removal of slaughterhouses and live-animal meat markets from the city of London was caused by a concern over tainted meat, particularly in view of epidemics like cholera and also to make the killing invisible so that it would not weigh on human conscience. In fact, it was claimed that such anti-cruelty measures were to elevate human beings and inculcate better public morals by promoting kind behaviour towards animals. Thus, the notion of animal welfare had many limitations, equivocations and exclusions.

Another aspect of the ambivalence in the concern for animal welfare was the menageries that sprang up from the 1820s. These were meant to be a symbol of progress and enlightenment of the emerging imperial world. The animals were exhibited as spoils of a growing empire and were supposed to imbue a sense of pride in imperialist activities. The animals were kept in narrow cages where they could not even turn around. One collection of large cats allowed visitors free admission if they brought a dog or a cat; they could watch it being fed to the lions. Sometimes dinners were hosted with exotic beasts on the menu. The serious scientific goal of studying animals, avowed by the Zoological Society of London (established in 1828) was certainly not the sole aim of such menageries.

Keith Thomas has pointed out the dichotomous development of human attitudes towards animals in early modern England.[16] Whereas in the medieval period animals were thought to have been created for the sole purpose of human exploitation, there emerged a 'modern sensibility' about nature, and hence about animals, leading to their appreciation and conservation. This occurred only after Europeans no longer felt at the mercy of nature, thanks to the rapid development of science and technology. In the premodern period, when cruelty to animals was condemned, it was not out of any genuine concern for animals but because it was believed to have a bestial impact on human character. These modern sensibilities generated the idea that it was unnatural for humans to take pleasure in cruelty. Still, the dominant view was that 'man stood to animals as did heaven to earth, soul to body, culture to nature'. Hence, this animality was something to be conquered by man, including the animality within humans themselves. During this time, people considered inferior—women, the insane, the Irish, American Indians, Africans, the poor and all colonized people—were all associated with animality.[17]

Needless to say, human attitude to animals have historical and cultural variations. This becomes quite clear even if we consider the most cared-for species, i.e. pets, throughout history. The preference for types of pets has varied from one culture to another and shifted over time. Cats and dogs are the most common pets, but in certain contexts monkeys, squirrels, tortoises, birds, fish and so on have also been domesticated and valued as pets. Japanese children love keeping insect as pets, which is probably linked to the traditional Japanese miniaturization of nature. Cats were objects of worship in ancient Egypt but were linked to witchcraft by the Catholic Church in thirteenth-century Europe and subjected to terrible torture. Then, once again, in the eighteenth century, they were seen in a positive light, particularly as Queen Victoria was known to be a cat lover. Popularity of certain dog breeds is determined by advertisements and changing fashions. Although popular almost everywhere, dogs are never kept as pets in Arab countries because they are considered unclean by the Koran.[18] Even the conceptual boundary between humans and animals, like that between culture and nature, is not universal. In many non-Western societies, nature is not a category opposed to culture and there are even societies without animals as a distinct category of beings, where boundaries between humans and animals are fluid. Such societies consider animals as persons or think of humans as capable of being metamorphosed into animals and vice versa. China is one such example. Carla Nappi, who has explored the shifting borders between animals and humans in early modern China, focuses on the changing classification of humanoid beasts (yetis), wild women, monkeys and other inhabitants of the human–animal borderland. She argues that in the past, there was a relative fluidity between human and animal categories, which disappeared in the modern age.[19] But even in such societies a hierarchy of value seems to exist with regard to humans and animals. Actually everywhere human attitudes to animals are full of dichotomies and ambivalence.

As mentioned previously, a comprehensive history of human–animal relationships in the context of India is yet to be written. The veneration of cows is often cited as proof of Hindu love for animals. However, this veneration does not extend to other animals. Foreign travellers like Marco Polo and Francois Bernier saw a utilitarian rationale behind the reverence for cows, as they contributed to the agrarian economy. At the same time, such travellers noted the existence of animal hospitals (*pinjrapols*) even for animals that were not 'useful'.[20] This, to them, was sheer charity, though perhaps a selfish motive of acquiring *punya* (virtue that would enable people to be happy in the afterlife) was also operative. Surely kindness did not predominate the human attitude to animals in India. Cruel animal sports like cock-fighting and big game-hunting were quite common in the subcontinent in the premodern period.

In the modern period, as industrial growth was impeded in India due to colonial rule, medieval relationships of relative intimacy between humans and animals largely continued here into the modern times as well—those between a peasant and his ox, between a shepherd and his flock, between a warrior and his war horse/elephant, and of course, between a human being and the ubiquitous dog. But modern ideas too gradually made their way into India from the colonial metropolis and scholars have shown how these ideas, harnessed to the imperial need, were full of contradictions and led to conflicts of interests between the colonizers and the colonized. For example, the British attitude regarding hunting was fraught with internal inconsistencies and often clashed with the indigenous people's idea of fairness.[21] Hunting was, of course, a major colonial sport and played a big role in colonial identity-formation as it was considered integral to the masculinity and the superiority of the British—in contrast with the animal-worshipping, vegetarian Indians. The British perceived Indian vegetarianism as proof of the effeminate nature of Hindu men. British attitude to animals was part of their rationale to justify colonial rule, while many Hindus among the colonized mobilized resistance to British rule by organizing cow protection.[22]

For animals in everyday life, compassion and science came to share a common cause, just as in the West. The British government's protectionism was geared towards preserving imperial interests. The educated Indians, known as the bhadralok in Bengal, imbibed from Europe the modern sensibilities regarding animals on the one hand and became aware of the threat to human health from sick animals on the other. New notions of social hygiene, environmental pollution, dietary balance and vegetarianism emerged. However, the bhadralok were typically caught between modernity and tradition, i.e. between modern science, local practices and a pride for the classical Hindu past in their attitude to animals, which was highly ambivalent in general. In 1861 the Calcutta Society for Prevention of Cruelty to Animals was founded. Its main purpose was 'not merely to prevent cruelty towards dumb animals by deterrent influence of legal punishment, but also to foster those merciful impulses that tended to the growth of humanity'.[23] The colonial government and upper-class Indians shared common concerns for founding a moral public order in colonial Calcutta regarding this matter and there was an increasing demand for kindness to animals. At the same time, both sought to preserve their own interests and were more anxious to discipline the lower-classes and the uneducated population in this respect than to actually help animals. Class divisions ran deep in Indian society just as in the West. Thus, all such measures reflected the existing class/race divisions rather than an urge to protect animals. The first Act of Prevention of Cruelty to Animals was passed in 1869. It was restricted to draft and sport animals used by Indians and did not refer to animals used in science research or British sports. Veterinary institutes developed after some time, with the Belgachia Veterinary College (1896) being the first. In 1900, the hospital attached to the college became an infirmary, and the Prevention of Cruelty to Animals Act was also passed. However, this also reflected a form of selective benevolence, as animals receiving treatment in Belgachia were categorized according to their utility, draft animals topping the priority list, followed by cattle, cats and dogs; then came Class III animals like sheep and goats.

In her doctoral research, Samiparna Samanta has focused on the handling of cattle plague, the concern for the condition of slaughter houses and the issue of overloading draft animals in colonial Bengal to show that each of these issues revolved around animals as mere proxy protagonists, revealing the utilitarian nature of colonial animal protection and the complex fault lines in colonial society.[24] The protective legislations were never applicable to merchants, traders and British cattle owners, but only to uneducated cart drivers, butchers, peasants and labourers. Different groups of people clashed on these issues and there was an uneasy cross-fertilization of tropes between the ethical, the religious and the scientific. Samanta also stresses that neither the discourse of the colonizers nor that of the colonized was monolithic, as there were various strands within each of them based on ideological, class and other differences. In fact, the two often overlapped. Despite some commendable works like that of Samanta, the shifts and ambiguities in the attitude to animals in Indian history await further studies.

Division and Differentiation, or Connection and Continuum?

There has been no systematic study in India when it comes to the history of thoughts and theories regarding animals, which is associated with general cultural attitudes. However, Western thoughts are generally accused of speciesism and insensitivity to animals and this is often contrasted with Oriental thoughts. Let us now explore how Western thoughts have evolved with regard to animals, particularly in modern times. Towards the end of the chapter we will see how Indian thoughts compare to Western thoughts.

Western thought predominantly upheld that human beings are superior to the rest of the animal kingdom.[25] Of its two most important roots, Judaism and Greek philosophy, the former projects God as approving of man's domination over other animals and proclaiming in Genesis that every living being should be man's food; in the latter school of thought, even though Pythagoras believed in transmigration of souls, he encouraged men to respect animal life and was a vegetarian himself, the dominant school of Plato and Aristotle laid emphasis on man's rationality and claimed that animals with less capacity for reasoning existed for the sake of man.

Christianity carried the legacy of such thoughts, eventually having an effect on the cultural conditions of the Roman Empire, which was more congenial for cultivation of martial skills than virtues of compassion and sympathy for the feeble and helpless. The Romans had games where even human beings were thrown inside the cages of wild animals. All animals and some human beings, particularly prisoners of war, criminals, etc., were considered unworthy of compassion (with the exceptions like Ovid, Seneca and Plutarch who urged people to treat animals with kindness). From the Christian point of view, man alone has an immortal soul and only human life is valuable. St. Thomas Aquinas also doubted the possibility of man, with his superior rationalism, having sympathetic feelings towards animals. However, when passion was under consideration, he asserted that even animals were sensitive to pain and hence humans should not treat them cruelly. Another argument of Aquinas was that if we are cruel to animals, we might also be cruel to human beings. This was similar to a view propagated by Christianity: treat animals kindly to secure your own place in heaven.

With the advent of the Renaissance, the form of humanism that emerged concerned man alone. This was followed by the Enlightenment and the emergence of modern science, and the killing animals on a large scale by way of experimentation was central to its development. Sir Francis Bacon justified this in support of the inductive logic of science (arriving at the truth of something by observing individual instances) and ultimately in the name of increasing the power of humanity. The seventeenth-century philosopher René Descartes tried to justify his deductive method (having a general understanding before one comprehends individual instances, that is, having a big picture and then working down) worsened the situation. His arguments ran thus: 'What is important is who is doing the observing. It is me. Now, who am I? Is it a body? Or am I just dreaming that I have a body?' This lead to the famous Cartesian saying: 'I am, because I think—my ability to think is the only thing I cannot doubt—because doubting is a form of thinking'. This dualism separated mind from body— 'I am my mind'—and had a massive impact on the way humans perceived animals. Animals function not through their minds, but through bodily organs; all they have is instinct. They do not know the world and do not have reason. They are like machines, mere automatons that cannot experience pain. This became a philosophical excuse for animal experiments. It was now not just faith in human domination, but a fact of science that justified scientific experimentation on animals as it was reasoned that we humans are superior, because we have something that the animals do not and that lack must be used to our benefit for this faunal world is physically the same, but mentally wholly different. A laboratory animal stands for a body that cannot feel pain. The mass use of animals to further scientific progress could thus be seen as one of modernity's most characteristic practices. Man, the cultured creature, was supposed to be a free-thinking subject, increasingly asserting his rights in the realm of politics, while animals remained mute objects or quasi-objects in the realm of nature. Even if they had a will, they could not express it. They can even be offered up as sacrifice in praise of the creator. It has been pointed out that species difference was foundational in structuring the liberal political institutions of modernity. As Thomas Hobbes' social contract theory stated, animals remained in the state of nature and outside this contract, hence men could kill them with impunity. Interestingly, the discourse of animality could be invoked against marginalized humans as well, who were not considered fully human, such as colonized people, slaves, blacks, and women.

However, scientific experiments during this period revealed striking resemblances between human and animal physiology. That animals did suffer and deserved some consideration had to be recognized. And even if it is just bodily sufferings, it could not be denied that body and bodily pain is important for all creatures. This created some discomfort. If one stated that animals suffered in the same way as humans and yet continued to experiment, then it was unethical. If one insisted that the animals are unlike us and that they do not experience the world the way humans do, and yet continue to experiment upon them, then the experiment is inaccurate, which is illogical.[26] Thus, during the Enlightenment era, David Hume expressed his view that humans were bound by the laws of humanity to treat animals gently. As religious dogmas began to be questioned during this period, it became possible for Voltaire to make a comparison between Christian practices and Hindu practices and condemn the former. Both Voltaire and Jean-Jacques Rousseau disparaged flesh-eating, though they themselves were not vegetarians. Immanuel Kant, who believed that each human had an intrinsic worth, did not think in similar terms when it came to non-humans. Jeremy Bentham denounced man's domination over animals as tyranny. He drew parallels between White man's treatment of Black slaves and man's treatment of animals. But he had very little influence. Hence the failure of the British Parliament to provide legal protection to animals in the early nineteenth century. Only some half-hearted measures could be taken in this direction, which have been noted in the previous section. On the other hand, the equation in the Judeo-Christian tradition between man's divine soul and logos, the uniquely human capacity for language, remained strong. Neuroscience too asserted in this period that human brains showed the vast difference between the nature of a brute and that of a man.[27] One implication of this was the thought that man could be human only to the degree that he transcended/mastered whatever animality he had within him.

These views again started changing soon. From the eighteenth century onwards, the sense of separation between man and other beings started breaking down. The 'Great Chain of Being' was the sacred phrase of this century. This was a classical conception of the cosmological order in which all beings, from lowest to highest, are hierarchically linked to form one interconnected whole. The conceptualization of the 'Great Chain of Being' can be traced back to Aristotlean or even pre-Aristotelian thoughts. As men became more inclined to see themselves as part of nature, they felt a sort of kinship with animals. But there was still a hierarchy, and the idea of man's supremacy was still prevalent.

However, Charles Darwin's seminal works *The Origins of Species* (1859) and *The Descent of Man* (1871) challenged the notion of the divine plan of creation and proved that man and other animals have a common origin. This had a tremendous impact upon man's attitude towards animals. The evolutionary theory reminded men of their inseparability with animals. Men could no longer claim that they had been created in the image of God and were different from animals. However, Darwin's theory was not easily accepted by many people. Moreover, 'Social Darwinism', an aberration of Darwin's thought, interpreted the idea of fitness in the phrase 'survival of the fittest' as aggression on others rather than adaptability to environment. Thus, it sought to explain the prevalent perceptions of inferiority and superiority in terms of evolution and also justified some people's exercise of power over others. Only, the power no longer came from God, but from nature.

This justified domination by humans of animals as well as other human beings. Therefore, even with the changes in the theoretical understanding of animal nature, humans continued to inflict pain on animals. Usually some excuse or other was made up to justify the continuation of earlier practices. Even Darwin did not sign a petition urging the Royal Society for the Prevention of Cruelty to Animals to press for legislative control of experiments on animals. Humans give importance to the animals only when their interests do not clash with the latter. Having said this, Darwin's ideas did make humans appear closer to animals and vice versa, which destabilized boundaries in both directions and had a far-reaching impact on human thought.

Emergence of Animal Rights Movements and Animal Studies

We have already mentioned the discourses of the Frankfurt school regarding animals, which was one of the early works in this area. Gradually, the theological debate on whether animals had a soul, was translated into the vocabulary of rights, with the animal rights movement emerging. The movement's foundational works were Peter Singer's seminal book *Animal Liberation* (1975) and, later, Tom Regan's *The Case for Animal Rights* (1983),[28] where 'speciesism' (supporting the cause of one's own species only and orienting all of one's thoughts accordingly, which we usually find among humans and also refer to as anthropocentricism) was likened to racism and sexism. Singer stressed on the capacity of animals to feel pain and presented this as a valid justification for saving their lives. Parallel to the animals rights movement inspired by Singer, there emerged a field of animals studies, becoming a distinct branch of humanities and social sciences from the 1980s.[29] Within this field, a number of scholars have tried to understand what different religious, philosophical and social traditions have to say about this issue.[30] Cruelty towards animals was also investigated in the context of various cultures and their related behavioural psychology.[31] There also emerged studies with more pronounced ethical and political concerns. Scholars discussed whether we as humans should draw a boundary at the species barrier in our ethical systems, whether we should treat non-human animals in their own rights or as mere means to our end. A number of works advocating vegetarianism can be cited as well.[32] Animal studies became a new poststructuralist area of cultural studies like feminist scholarship or queer studies in 1990s, following race and gender studies as well as postcolonial studies of the 1970s and 1980s (with the two early landmarks of Frantz Fanon's *Wretched of the Earth*, 1968 and Edward Said's *Orientalism*, 1978). Animal studies was like them interdisciplinary in nature. Sciences such as ecology, cognitive ethology and primatology have contributed a great deal to this area. *Primate Visions* (1989) by Donna Haraway, a biologist and a feminist, is considered a pioneering work in this area. A new kind of animal history has emerged as well, pioneered by Erica Fudge, which attempts to treat animals not as mere objects but to bring out their side of history. This theoretical and critical space has been enriched by Gilles Deleuze, Félix Guattari, Martin

Heidegger, Jacques Derrida and Giorgio Agamben. Interest in literary circles, such as in the creative works of J.M. Coetzee, Timothy Findley and other writers, reflecting on human–animal relationships, has facilitated the development of animals studies too.[33] Postcolonialism often questions the dehumanizing drive of colonialism and its brutal impact on both humans and animals. *Postcolonial Ecocriticism* by Graham Huggan and Helen Tiffin depicts the intersectionality between species, race, queerness and gender without prioritizing humans over animals.[34] Such scholarly works with different foci feed into each other, attempting to reinterpret man's history of violence and make animals visible in academics in order to overcome a long period of blindness. This is very often a politicized exercise, in a similar vein to other poststructuralist and postcolonial studies. There is also a burgeoning area of animal rights law at the intersection of philosophy and legal studies, led by scholars like Gary Francione and Steven M. Wise. However, on the whole, scholars involved in animal studies considerably differ in their attitudes to animals and have rarely departed from anthropocentricism, which is of course very difficult for any human to do. Not all have an agenda of protectionism, though some have entered moral and political debates forthrightly. Donna Haraway, a pioneering name in the field, has a complex attitude in this regard. She allows moral and political questions about both people and animals to remain in the picture while articulating positions that are not likely to satisfy either animal rights activists or those who protest that the animal rights movement has imposed hardships on communities dependent on hunting and fishing. Indeed, there are scholars who have urged us to replace ethics with aesthetics with regard to animals, to appreciate the aesthetic value of animality and thus to remove the actual living, breathing beings from discussion. Marc R. Fellenz argues that we should hunt animals as this is a Paleolithic drive and the natural human condition prevailed in the Paleolithic period: 'The yearning the hunter feels for the animal is not merely the desire to capture, but to become—to exploit one's full humanity by experiencing that part of it that is akin to the animal.'[35] However, this seems to be an extreme position. We will now take a brief look at some sub-disciplines, themes, and arguments of the increasingly expanding disciplinary field of animal studies.[36]

Behaviourism, Ethology and Other Sciences

Let us first consider some scientific disciplines like behaviourism, primatology and ethology that started emerging as distinct fields from the 1930s and devoted themselves to study of animals. New attitudes emerged alongside new knowledge and this ultimately had philosophical ramifications that resonated in postmodernism, postcolonialism and, eventually, posthumanism. What intrigued all these fields is whether or not non-human animals had emotion and intelligence. No easy consensus could emerge on this, because, after all, animals cannot speak and hence it is difficult to access their minds. That animals can feel pain and pleasure was clear. But for a long time it was argued that these are just innate responses, not emotions. An animal seemed to be like a machine that had no part in its own life. It was thought to be controlled partly by instincts that it had acquired in the process of evolution and was genetically determined by outside conditions. Behaviourism dominated the field prior to the rise of sciences such as ethology, and the former's interpretation of animal behaviour tended to favour a kind of minimalism, which would only ascribe to an animal the minimum capability that could explain a behaviour; anything more than this was seen as unwarranted anthropomorphism. Even Konard Lorenz and Niko Tinbergen, who tried to understand animal minds, tended to objectify them with the instinct theory. Why should humans postulate consciousness and all its near-human implications in animals to explain some behaviour?—this was what behaviourists (and their 'instinctivist' brethren) used to ask. But of course, extreme behaviourists argued that even human feelings were merely hard-wired responses to external stimuli.

Nowadays, however, a lot of research is being done on animal cognition, language, tool use, sexuality, etc. It is said that emotions arise in the brain or the limbic system, which humans share with other mammals as well as many other species. That an animal's capacity for pain, fear and other similar responses are needed for survival is now a generally accepted theory. Thus, it is claimed that emotionality is a morally relevant psychological state shared by humans and non-humans. Still, non-human emotion is not treated at par with human emotion. Even today, the *Oxford Companion to Animal Behaviour*, a standard reference work, advises animal behaviourists that 'One is well advised to study [an animal's] behaviour, rather than attempting to get at any underlying emotion.' An animal may make certain movements and sounds, and show certain brain and chemical signals when its body is damaged in a particular way. But the dominant belief still is that this does not mean that an animal 'feels' pain as we do. It is claimed that animals are merely programmed to act in a certain way based on stimuli. But, of course, this question can be asked of a human as well. Many scientists regard all emotions and cognition, in humans and animals alike, as having a purely mechanistic basis.

Primates, in particular great apes, have highly developed capabilities for empathy, as theories of mind reveal. Great apes also have complex social systems. Young apes and their mothers have very strong bonds of attachment. When a baby chimpanzee dies, its mother exhibits mournful behaviour. Even in the case of magpies, there are instances in which they not only mourn the death of a fellow magpie, they even bring back grass and lay it by the corpse—a definite ritual-like behaviour, which is a sort of culture! Dogs have been observed to have different personality traits. Some develop depression and even break down easily in adverse situations, some can handle unpleasant situations better—a kind of variation humans show as well. Even fish have different personalities. Observation of a group of trout, for example, has revealed that some of them are more willing than others to take risks. Some are more social than others, while some fish prefer being alone. They also have different preferences as far as eating habits are concerned. During his lifetime, Darwin had also focused on individual variations among animals.[37] Indeed, each animal is an individual, just like each human.

The major barrier that scientists have faced while looking for animal emotion and intelligence is their lack of language, at least their inability to communicate with us. In fact, it is precisely their lack of language that was once regarded as the defining difference between humans and animals. It was Descartes' contention that because animals could not speak, they had no reason at all. ('How unreasonable!', one must say). But there have also been experiments on the possibility of animals communicating with humans. Parrots can repeat noises, though it is argued that this is like a human infant who repeats noises without understanding their meaning. Sometimes, an animal is made to communicate through different types of language—sign language, symbolic language, etc. They often seem to understand meaningful words and even sentences and respond accordingly. This perhaps gives us a glimpse into the otherwise impenetrable interior of the animal mind. Penny Patterson's gorilla Koko is a famous example. She even expressed grief about the death of her favourite kitten through a form of sign language. The gap between species may thus be closing within the fields of science, but a great deal of skepticism about this prevails. Doesn't an animal merely respond to their master's body language in such cases, taking up cues or following the prompts of its teacher. Was it not the teacher who made the animal signs meaningful?

A number of scholars are now trying to approach the matter differently. They are inverting the original question 'Can animals learn to speak human language?' Fudge argues that perhaps Koko had an interior life, and if she had a control over it, she might not choose to live in San Fransisco. If we could hear animals speak, we might not want to hear what they have to say. Maybe they are smarter than we are. After all, how many of us can speak Gorilla![38] This undercuts the notion of our inbuilt superiority that has persisted in much of language research. The untranslatability of animal languages may not be a failure on their part; rather, it calls for a recognition that human language is not the only language, and that we do not have the monopoly on meaning. We must remember that animals can communicate within their species perfectly well—of course, they cannot easily communicate with us, but we cannot easily communicate with them either.

A way out of this conundrum could involve the observation of animals in their own habitats, as is common in primatology. But even this has been criticized as 'simian orientalism' (by Haraway, following Said's *Orientalism*)[39]—construction of the 'self' from the raw material of the 'other', which connects animal studies with postcolonial studies. It is argued that far from being an objective science, such efforts made by primatologists are linked with the discourses of colonialism, racism and patriarchy. The ideas of race, gender, etc., as being innate as well as the bases of inferiority/superiority has been challenged over the past few decades as a construct of Eurocentric and androcentric culture. Similarly, it has been argued that animality is a human construct that removes our 'civilized' species from the 'natural' world of animals. It reveals the human failure to look beyond itself, to achieve the desirable objectivity for understanding animals. Animals are blind spots in human knowledge in which the world's axis turns on the humans. Our taxonomy of animals is an example. As Friedrich Nietzsche pointed out:

If I make up the definition of a mammal, and then after inspecting a camel, declare 'look, a mammal', I have indeed brought a truth to light in this way, but it is a truth of limited value. That is to say, it is a thoroughly anthropomorphic truth which contains not a single point which would be truth in itself, or really or universally valid apart from man.[40]

Ethology on the other hand is interested in animals for their own sake. Judge them according to their own rule, and not that of the human observers, it seems to say. Animal behaviour is to be understood and given meaning within the context of the animal world. But even here the question of objectivity arises. For example, doubts have been expressed about the use of words like 'childhood', 'adolescence', 'social structure', etc., with regard to chimpanzees. It is argued that such use ascribes human characteristics to non-humans and thus is a kind of anthropomorphism, which is an ethological sin. But then, as Fudge says, we poor humans do not have any alternative. We can only see what we see, and we can only describe what our language allows us to describe.

Animal studies are increasingly leading us to the reality of our own limited perspective. And some thinkers are urging us to get over it by being aware of it first. When Noam Chomsky pointed out the distinctness of grammar-based human language, some scholars raised objections. A chimpanzee called Nim Chimpsky was taught human language to prove Chomsky wrong. But despite the efforts of its trainer, the chimpanzee's skill of communication in human language did not seem quite adequate. However, one can perhaps raise the question, Why try to teach him our language at all? As Chomsky said 'If you want to study human, you study language. If you want to study pigeon you study their home instinct.' He urges us to look beyond our usual frame of reference. But in the case of pigeons, humans prefer to call it a homing 'instinct'—implying it is not learnt or acquired. In fact, the skill of pigeons is beyond human realms of classification, and hence we do not recognize it as a form of intelligence. Erica Fudge tauntingly says, 'It is as if the pigeon has no choice but to go home, whereas we can choose to get lost.'[41] The same can be said of a sniffer dog's ability—we would consider it natural capacity, not evidence of intelligence. But then what about guide dogs, trained to guide blind persons? These creatures even show 'intelligent disobedience', thus going beyond just taking cues from their masters. They tear down the boundary between humans and dogs by 'completing' a 'deficient' human.

All such scientific research points to similarity rather than difference between humans and animals. The similarity is based on the body, which is central to the history of life; even the mind is now known to be embedded in the body. The more developed an animal's automatic nervous system, the closer it is to humans in terms of emotions. We share our cognition and rationality, too, more or less with many mammals. This shift from theocentricism to biocentrism has indeed brought humans and non-humans contiguous and close to one another.[42] Maybe animals are more like us than we allow ourselves to imagine. Thus, it has been argued that the notion of anthropomorphism may not be used in a derogatory sense, if it allows us to recognize this. Maybe it is a positive way of recognizing the links and developing empathy. We sometimes say that a cat mother is so much like a human mother. Can we not also say that a human mother is so much like a cat mother? Should we not recognize the animal in humans too, instead of muting the animal in humans by adopting powerful cultural blinders, which we usually do?

In fact, ethologists have even found evidence of 'culture' in animals—culture as a way of life, a social world where we see behavioural transmission not resting on biological or ecological limitations and yet being passed from generation to generation. Intergenerational transmission of culture includes history as well. History is always regarded as a sort of civilization or culture (denied to the Africans by Hegel). We know of potato-washing by some Japanese monkeys, who thus made a transition from the raw to the cooked, which is a mark of culture according to Claude Lévi-Strauss. Moreover, cultural variations can be found between monkey communities—in grooming, courtship behaviours, etc. These are not just instinctive or natural, but created, i.e. cultural.

But of course, an animal's simpler mode of being is more natural than cultural, and each species is different from the other in many more ways. Hence, recognizing the similarities may not be enough; recognizing the differences too, albeit respectfully, is required. Instead of attempting to assess the animal's capacity to be like us, perhaps we should just try to understand them (and maybe learn from them a few things). Then we would find problems with our own sense of power and domination. The ape does not ape us, it is itself—very different and for that reason unique. Instead of thinking about them as failed humans, we can think of them as *themselves*, but perhaps not absolutely different from us. We are simultaneously tied to and separated from other animals. But we have gone beyond a simple recognition of differences and constructed them as 'others'; such otherization, even regarding humans, appear natural to us.

What seems to be the most important contribution of animal studies is that today some of the ways in which we used to assert our difference from animals are breaking down, thanks to considerable scientific research. There has emerged a new notion of animal intelligence, of their similarity to humans, as well as conceptions of the moral place of animals. Many agree that we should not look at animals through a human lens and view them as lacking in certain traits that are considered to be uniquely human, and also that hierarchical evaluation based on the differences of degree between humans and animals are not always correct.

But, as Fudge points out, such is our human culture that even the recognition of similarity cannot supersede our sense of superiority and urge for domination in real life. Hence, fox-hunting in England was conducted with the reasoning that the animal was wily, cunning and highly intelligent; hence it was a 'worthy opponent' and 'fair game', because it could escape the hunt. However, this is not really a powerful ethical claim as we tend to kill animals whether or not they are intelligent—an animal is an animal is an animal. This only emphasizes the confusions that persist in our relationships with animals. Sometimes our excuse is they are instinctual machines, and at other instances we would argue that they are clever subjects matching our intelligence. Our culture makes us insensitive to animals by promoting self-deceit. Animal studies thus reveals the ultimate irrationality and immorality of *Homo sapiens*.

Rethinking Animals as Subjects and Agents

Rethinking animals as subjects and agents is another big contribution of animal studies. Agency is a term that emerged in the 1970s from human studies as a critique of structuralism (which does not recognize conscious actions of individuals) and has become a key trope since then, albeit a contested one. Agency means cognitive abilities, self-awareness, interests, will, preferences, intentions and purposeful actions. Upholding the notion of agency in animal studies coincides with individualization and subjectification of animals and is conducted with a political agenda. The political ramification of these ideas is that a subject having agency should be protected. For a long time, subjecthood and agency were considered uniquely human attributes that were embedded in human exceptionalism; animals were not considered capable of either. Even if an animal was considered a subject, nobody believed that it could be a willful agent. And when its agency was somehow recognized, it was thought to be an agent without being a subject. Today, scholars know better; their studies reveal animal agency, particularly in the cases of vertebrate macro-organisms having feelings and empathy. Of course, these capacities can be perceived more in some animals than others. The more developed a creature's nervous system, the more agentive role it is likely to play. This agency is also likely to be associated with subjecthood as well. But even those with less developed nervous systems can perhaps be considered agents in a way—if we define the term 'agency' broadly. Perhaps they can be considered agents without being subjects. But we will return to this later.

First, let us take the word agency in its strictest sense, i.e. 'converting ideas into purposeful actions', and let us consider animals with developed nervous system to see how they act as agents. We often try to objectify such animals and deny them their agency with the instinct theory. But humans too are often driven by instinct, by our biological needs. Take predation, for example. Is the act of a tiger attacking a man a mere natural event? Does the tiger not act as an agent? Both wolves and humans are social hunters, often seeking the same prey in the same location, which may make confrontations inevitable. The animals that live on the edge between civilization and wilderness, at the intersection of the natural and the cultural, are thus more dangerous for humans. It is not difficult to see both human and non-human animals acting as agents in such situations. But, of course, then all animals, from mega-fauna to microbes, become key agents in the unfolding of life processes, driven by their biological needs, including hunger.

We have already seen how ethologists and behavioural psychologists apply a technical language that ultimately presents a mechanomorphic portrayal of animals—innately fixed action patterns released by appropriate stimulus. Moreover, they argue that if specific energies accumulate, even inappropriate stimulus can trigger such patterns. The case of a peacock dancing before a pig noted by Darwin can perhaps be thus explained. How does this relate to the question of agency? A scientist may argue that the dancing just happened to the peacock, that at best the peacock was a subject, not an agent. But perhaps one can view it differently. One can view even the pig differently, because the latter might have responded to the peacock in some way, out of its own volition. Can we not imagine these two beings liberated from pure utilitarian (read reproductive) motives, enjoying a creative, improvised action together? Indeed, Darwin, while describing this scene, said that the peacock 'evidently wishes for a spectator of some kind, and will shew off his finery, ... before even pigs'. And if we humans can say, '*Hriday amar nachere ajike mayurer mato nachere*' ('My heart is dancing today like a peacock', as the poet Rabindranath Tagore exclaimed at the onset of monsoon), can the pig not feel something akin to this too? Even if we are not sure about the pig, perhaps it should not be too difficult to grant agency at least to rethe peacock in this case. Perhaps we deny animals their agency because we do not understand them. People involved in social studies know well that human beings often do not even understand their fellow humans adequately and hence treat them unfairly and even cruelly—we only have to take note of specifically human issues of caste, communalism, colonialism, etc. Human understanding and treatment of animals is even more inadequate.

Animals' agency becomes more prominent when they resist or protest, which happens in the case of 'labouring others' among humans too, i.e. poor peasants and workers. We just have to recall the work of the Subalternists. Resistance is surely a vector of agency. Working animals often resist human activities, which credits them with full agency and also conveys their perspective on the situation. It has been shown that working animals like cows involved in the work with the breeders, are not really automatons, that they invest their intelligence and affects into their work, follow rules, cooperate with the master and anticipate actions. We usually take all this for granted and therefore do not see their work. We regard their cooperation as mechanistic. Their work becomes perceptible only when they refuse to cooperate (slow down pace, avoid work etc.). They are all 'secret agents', says Vinciane Despret in an article titled 'From Secret Agents to Interagency'.[43] And 'secret agents' often look like subjects through their acts of resistance. Agency is not independence but signifies the multiple ways one creature depends on others, human or non-human, always waiting to derive agency from others, something that feminist theory stresses today.

We can easily think of agency as something even more purposeful, full of reason and judgment, i.e. in terms of a more robust and calculating form of agency. Dogs, horses and some other animals can satisfy even such criteria as we know that they can be intensively trained. If one asks how much *agency* does training (and hence, being subject to the will of humans) leave them anyway, today social studies and researchers in the field of subaltern studies shows that even in a hierarchical relationship, even while doing another's will, an individual can become an agent. There are other species, much like humans, whose agency can be established rather easily. We know of many animals who do intentional acts of friendship, who grieve the loss of near and dear ones, or who take revenge on those that have wronged them. They are agents not just because they have impacted their own reality, but also because they display varying degrees of subjectivity and intentionality and are not solely governed by instinct. They are able to learn, use tools and form complex social bonds. Primates are, of course, closely related to humans, not only in their bipedalism and other physical features, but in many of their gestures, their practice of patriarchy and capitalism. Even a hungry domestic cat has a range of choices about how to procure food—jumping up onto the kitchen table to scavenge tidbits, pestering its owner, hunting moles in the garden. It makes a choice on its own regarding how to fulfill its hunger. Even if we choose to call it instinct, the cat settles its instinct through one of various ways.

But let us now think of agency in a very broad sense. In the above-mentioned article Despret suggests a shift in the meaning of the concept of agency. She actually prefers the term 'agencement', through which creatures of different species can become companion-agents. The word 'agencement' has an intimate link with agency, and yet never insists on an active process of attunement and is not something fixed. There is no agency without agencement, and agencement is co-animation by way of engaging, inciting, inspiring and so on. In this sense, one may become an agent without being a subject, nevertheless one is not an object when one goes through a process of agencement. If we thus recast our definition of agency, Bruno Latour's concept of 'actor-network theory'(ANT)[44] or Tim Ingold's 'organism-in-its-environment'[45] seem useful too. For Latour, a sort of agency exists in practically everything, because any given thing is involved in a vast range of interactions with other things. He argues that there can be two kinds of actors: intermediaries and mediators. Intermediaries transport meaning or force without changing things much whereas mediators are unreliable: 'their input is never a good predictor of their output'. These two options sum up the relationship of anything to another in any instance of doing or happening. An army, soldiers and horses alike, is an intermediary while a general is a mediator. According to ANT, nature and society/culture are not givens and not two distinct poles; they are created and to be explained by hybrid collectives of quasi-objects and quasi-subjects. Haraway also talks about companion-species and argues that species exist only in relation to one another: 'Beings do not pre-exist their relatings.'[46] If we realize this, we can recognize the agency of animals without being sentimental about them and without expecting human levels of agency (intentionality in particular) from them. In this sense, of course, even the microbes in our body—killer pathogens from small pox to influenza to Corona viruses—are examples of our shared intimacy with non-humans and they too have an agentive role.

A kind of romantic pantheism regarding animals has been in existence since a long time. Early environmentalism also revealed their importance in a way, i.e. by highlighting their utility for ecological balance. But today we are being beckoned towards a different approach. Recent scholarship has been moving in numerous, fairly radical ontological directions. Cary Wolfe in *What is Post-humanism?* urges an approach that sees the human as 'fundamentally a prosthetic creature that has co-evolved with various forms of technicity and materiality, forms that were radically "non-human" and yet have nevertheless made the human what it is'.[47] Wolfe, following Derrida, wants us to recognize the dynamic interaction of beings in patterns and systems, to understand how a non-human being can force a transformation in human being. This world is a fluid assembly of agents. It is an interconnected liveliness of all matters (which even the seventeenth-century philosopher Spinoza recognized). Today, scholars tend to consider agents as potential combinations rather than inevitably autonomous entities. The influence of Haraway, Deleuze and Guattari is decisive in this approach. But there is also much borrowed from the actor-network theory (ANT) of Bruno Latour. ANT is less passionate about the world and its value; 'less, well, pantheistic, but equally or even more focused on the minute but certain interactions and transformations that occur as one thing acts on another'.[48] Latour thus criticizes mainstream sociology's understanding of the social world, its prejudice towards finished human persons and human groups. After all, humans are agents only in the context of a particular situation and framework, but so are all other beings. Rationality is only one characteristic of our species; it does not drive all our actions. In many cases, conscious thought does not precede action. At the same time, non-humans, like humans, are capable of acting intentionally.

Humans are increasingly realizing that they are not the centre of the story of life. New understandings of artificial intelligence (AI), genetics and animal cognition challenge the sense of the human subject as separate from the rest of the world and establish that there is no human exceptionalism. If AI makes humans look like a rather inferior being in terms of intelligence, all we are left with is emotions, affects, will, etc., and, of course, with the will to live, which we share with our co-species on this planet. Scientists today are also making persuasive claims about animal rationality, consciousness and language. Thus, animals' role within networks of effects stares us in the face and we are urged to probe the particular character of animal engagement. Non-humans are mobile, feeling and thinking. They are not separate from humanity, but rather an intimate partner in the biological and historical journey of our species. They have the ability to shape contexts, they can make a difference in our lives and sometimes do so intentionally, though ANT downplays intentionality while considering agency. Some critics have accused Latour and others of levelling power relations between humans and non-humans by attributing equal capacities to both. However, his is a moral approach with a view to changing the course of history.

Human consciousness about the historical relevance of animal agency is on the rise. A new consciousness of the endangerment of charismatic fauna, loss of their usufruct rights, appropriation of their resources and the resultant tension, and divergent impact of technology on their lives is discernable. Rethinking animals as subjects and agents makes us remap human–animal boundaries in emotive as much in ecological terms. This is leading to a new kind of animal history. Animals' historical roles, manifesting various degrees and levels of agency, is widespread within the network of effects. If so, history can at least try to throw light on the agency of many more such animals. 'Given one theory of agency or another, animals deserve a place in that necessarily human story.'[49]

Writing Animals into History and Anthropology

Animals permeate our history and we theirs, because we share the world with them. Yet, they have long been neglected in the history written by humans. By largely erasing animals from historical accounts, historians reinforce the narrative of the nature-culture split, instead of historicizing and challenging it. Things have, however, recently started changing.

For a long time, historians believed (and some of them still do) that history began when humans ceased to be animals, i.e. when biology gave way to culture. By this logic, it was impossible to include animals in history. However, they could sometimes be held within the embrace of natural history/evolutionary history. The American Museum of Natural History, for example, prominently displayed the natural history of horses, illustrating profound changes in the body size as different equine species adapted to different ecological niches, also showing how the original three-toed horses lost two of their digits. But historians did not think of including animals in the history that they wrote, the history of civilization that dates back to not more than 5,000 years, at most to the inception of agriculture about 10,000 years ago.

Common sense sometimes gave recognition to the central role of animals in human history. One may cite sayings like 'For want of a nail, the horse shoe was lost; for want of the shoe, the horse was lost; for want of a horse, the kingdom was lost'.[50] or 'A history of England without cattle is something like a history of global capitalism without the Internet.' But acknowledging only this, i.e. treating animals as objects, is not really animal history. It is imperative to go into further depth, highlighting their agency or at least agencement in view of the web of 'inextricable affinities' sketched above.

There was a time when history encompassed only the accounts of great men and was a political power narrative. This broadened into social history, which led to inclusion of more human actors, particularly subaltern categories (peasants, workers and other underdogs). Historians also tried to retrieve the latter's subjecthood as far as possible. Our ideas about proper subjects of history have thus changed. And pushing the same logic further, there has been a slow movement towards taking animals more seriously. Environmental and ecological history was the first sub-discipline that broadened historical agency to include natural forces. Animals are part of nature, hence a kind of agent, and thus seemed important historical players in environmental history. From the mid-1970s, animals started occupying an important place in environmental history. Alfred Crosby's *The Columbian Exchange* (1972) and W.H. McNeill's *Plagues and Peoples* (1976) are well-known examples. There are many creatures that have derived biological advantage by allying themselves with *Homo sapiens*, thereby asserting their agency. Many of them act outside the realm of the human consciousness, but they have established an ecological intimacy with humans. One such example is that of the Japanese beetle, which were stowed away in bundles of azaleas (a kind of flowering shrub), and shipped to New Jersey one day, where they thrived. Today, we are well aware of how organisms like pigs, sheep, cows, dogs, etc., acted as allies of imperialism, devoured native crops, transformed landscapes of the New World, introduced obnoxious weeds there, etc. Cattle replaced bison on the American frontier, microparasites transported from the wool of imported sheep to llama and alpaca devastated them and English mastiffs chased Indians from newly established plantations. Indeed, as Crosby shows, as the number of humans declined, population of imported animals shot upwards in the New World.[51] In the American context, horses and dogs acted in aid of European imperialism. In this sense, they were agents; but they were agents also in a more profound sense. They did this because they had their own agendas to attend to—eating, reproducing, rummaging. We may also think of mosquitos and malaria that devastated Bengal in the colonial period in a similar manner. Indeed, J.R. McNeil has invested 'revolutionary mosquito's with 'agency' in the process of empire-building and revolution in the Greater

Caribbean.[52] W.H. McNeill's *Plagues and Peoples* shows how microparasites were transferred from livestock to humans and heavily impacted history.[53]

That perceptions of animals are linked to different historical conditions of people has been revealed by a number of historians. Human attitude to animals in different historical contexts are currently being explored. As mentioned previously, Keith Thomas' *Man and the Natural World* (1983) depicted in great detail the early modern British attitude to animals. In France, Robert Delort's book *Les animaux ont une histoire* (1984) was more radical and tried to present an animal-centred perspective. Princeton's Davis Centre published a selection of essays in 1997, which eventually became a book: Angela Creager and William Jordan edited *The Animal-Human Boundary: Historical Perspectives* (Rochester, 2002). Virginia DeJohn Anderson's *Creatures of Empire: How Domestic Animals Transformed Early America* (2004) is a well-known book. And then Mark Stoyle's *The Black Legend of Prince Rupert's Dog: Witchcraft and Propaganda during the English Civil War* (2011) further normalized animals within historiography by linking a social climate and a political movement through an animal. But all these works seem to be just the beginning of the field of animal studies as an increasingly rich history of animals is being promised today.

Granting animals subjecthood and willful agency and looking at issues from animals' perspectives may seem difficult but some historians are trying even this. They argue that human perspective is not the true and only perspective possible. Indeed, they know that humanity itself contains multiple 'others' and there is no single human perspective on something, which postmodernism and cultural relativism have made us aware of.[54] Human beings are not a homogenous category with a single history. Furthermore, humans of the past are not the same as humans of today. Still, in history, we often try to assume a continuum. We try to 'go beyond the impossibility of the longing to speak with the dead'.[55] After all, one is restricted to the resources of one's own mind and, hence, it is difficult for one to go beyond one's own subjective position. Still, historians try to realize what might it be like to be another person in a given situation in the past. As Marc Bloch argues in *The Historian's Craft*, we have an immediate awareness of only our own mental state of this moment (even our own sensory experiences cannot be retrieved once they are gone; a taste or a smell cannot be experienced in the same way as when we first experience it). In this respect, 'a student of present is scarcely better off than the historian of the past'.[56] For Bloch, history is, like life itself, an exercise in limitation.

Getting over human essentialism through a process of empathetic insights (as far as possible, based on similarities between humans and nonhumans) and sympathetic projection, a historian might try to recover the animals' own perspective in historical studies. Even if materials are not adequate for this, s/he can at least ask new questions by way of addressing the animal world and its past. Let us explore how Erica Fudge has done this to understand cows and their relationship with humans in early modern England, in a seventeenth-century village in north

Essex to be more precise.[57] She takes her cue from a single-line entry in an Essex Sessions Roll about Elizabeth Elsing, 'a woman of idle and disorderly life, a milker of other men's beasts', who had been put in a house of correction and was now released. The legal indictment listed Elsing's crimes in terms of the economic value of the milk she had stolen. Fudge, however, thinks of her criminality in terms of how her milking might have affected the cows involved. What it was like to be a cow being milked by a stranger? She tries to answer this question with help from the American animal scientist Temple Gardin, who claimed that she could comprehend a cow's view of the world better because of her autism (based on this, Temple redesigned slaughterhouses in America to improve the experience of cows as they were being led to their death). Unfamiliar sights and sounds are frightening for cows. Being milked by a stranger, like Elsing, must have been terribly unsettling for the cows. An individual cow knew her milker, a recognition which was reinforced by regular interactions and friendliness. Fudge has also talked about the possible longer-term impact of the theft on the physiology of the cow, which may have caused health problem and reduction of milk supply for the family, and in turn had detrimental effect on the family's health (apart from its economic condition).

Similarly, David Gary Shaw raises the following question:[58] In the Napoleonic wars, especially the Battle of Waterloo, the Duke of Wellington acted as an agent, but what about his horse Copenhagen? Shaw tries to understand Copenhagen's agency based on an anecdote of resistance put up by the horse. Of course, the horse did not know the details of the war he was involved in. But such details may have been opaque to many humans, including ordinary soldiers. Even Wellington had inaccurate information and inadequate understanding of his own forces' deployment. Acting centres are often myopic and scholars stress the unidirectionality of history. Posthumanism argues that perhaps we should abandon notions of agency that begin with the assumption of the specialness of reason, that of the human in particular. Rather than agency's intellectual relevance, animal studies pays more attention to broadly hedonistic concerns—agency generated by hunger, suffering and pains of animals. We also tend to act as agents even when we miss the mark we intended. The intention or purpose itself seems crucial for agency. But can we attribute any purpose to Wellington's horse?

Wellington and the horse went to war as a unit and fought together. A record says that at the end of the penultimate day of the battle, at around 11 p.m., when Wellington was handing the horse over to his groom, the animal kicked out, as if untired and still in battle readiness—a kick that almost killed the duke. The next day, on the day of the Battle of Waterloo, as Wellington dismounted Copenhagen after about eighteen hours, he again gave the duke a playful kick. But what did the horse mean by this? Such an act has been interpreted as the horse showing his high spirits, but one narrator has argued that he was angry. Shaw interprets it as subaltern resistance. Given his training and sense of discipline the horse could not show this on the battlefield, but when it was no longer in the context of the battle, i.e. when he was in his stable, his own territory, he dared to behave differently. The timing of these acts is important too. Most of our doings—of people and animals alike—are habituated, copied and even instinctual. Of course, there is reason for these habits. But we have to take the sharp edges off deliberative reason to understand that a horse or a dog could possess meaningful agency. The Duke rode Copenhagen the whole day and the horse did not kick him then. He decided to let the Duke ride him. He was compliant, his agency congruent with Wellington's agency. Both were actants operating within a network. Shaw also points out evidence that Copenhagen was not easy to ride, which was claimed by people other than the duke. The predictability of Copenhagen in battlefield was 'not because he was more of an automaton than another horse, but because the matching up, the training, the character, the experience, was more carefully and comfortably executed'.[59] Agency thus differs within as well as between species.

Likewise, Chris Pearson[60] presented a story of the war dogs on the Western front during the First World War, and shows with the help of canine psychology how they displayed some degree of intentionality and self-directed action. Of all companion-species, dogs lay bare most forcefully the fiction of the human–animal divide. Dogs and humans have shaped each other for centuries. They are not only integral parts of and shapers of human societies, they have helped us become 'human'. On the Western front, soldiers and dogs worked together to uncover danger, carry supplies and news, and locate wounded soldiers. Reports surfaced of individual dogs acting on their own 'initiative'. Messenger dogs could travel large distances independently and successfully deliver messages against all odds (though some such stories are undoubtedly exaggerated and stuff of legends). Messenger dogs often learnt from one another and warned or helped humans without being instructed to do so. Dogs made a difference to the conduct of the war. Of course, they were unaware of the war's political or social contexts but, it can be argued, so were many human soldiers.

A military-dog training school was established in Britain in 1916. Like police dog-training manuals, military ones too asserted that trainers needed to understand canine characteristics in a thorough and logical way and respond skillfully to canine psychology. However, not all dogs behaved in ways that their trainers intended; some were branded as disobedient. Pearson argues that rather than dismissing the training manuals as anthropocentric statements, we can read them to gain some insights into dogs' agency. Of course, human-canine power relations were uneven. Thousands of dogs were injured or killed in the war, or were put down for being disobedient. But cross-species communication and bonds also persisted. Pet-keeping offered the company amusement and an emotional outlet. It is said that even the hardest soldiers softened in front of their animals. Dogs humanized the front and kept soldiers from feeling lonely at night. In this way, by drawing on canine psychology, we can perhaps write dogs into the history of wars. Though this will not be history from animals' point of view, it will be history written with animals in mind.

Talking about war dogs, one also remembers the story of Bobby,[61] a dog that Emmanuel Levinas met as a prisoner in the camps of Nazi Germany. The dog showed up regularly during the morning and evening assemblies, cheerfully barking and jumping. When the prisoners were denied human status by the guards, Bobby was the only creature who made them feel alive and human. Again, this is not a story that enters the mind of the animal concerned. But it is a compelling tale that shows humans and dogs as fellow creatures between whom a deep bond is possible, something that human beings often deny to other humans. Maybe we run the risk of romanticizing dogs in this way, but are we not inclined towards somewhat romanticizing peasants while researching peasants' history as well? It seems we are inclined towards either demonizing or romanticizing beings whom we do not quite understand.

As far as the history of animals or of human–animal relationships in the Indian context is concerned, some interesting works have been produced recently. We have already discussed some of them to sketch the history of human attitude to animals. We have seen how some scholars have tried to understand British colonialism and the relationship between the British and natives through the lens of animals. The cow is a species that has attracted some scholarly attention. There are studies exploring how colonial rule had a catastrophic impact on Indian cattle cultures in various regions,[62] or how cow protection became a rallying symbol of political mobilization.[63] A number of works have also been written on hunting practices,[64] investigating the contests over game, forests and wilderness. Samiparna

Samata has examined the discourses of cruelty against animals in Bengal between 1850 and 1920, focusing on the epizootic of 1864 as well as slaughterhouses and animals as beasts of burden and showing the animals were signifiers of race, gender, class and suchlike relations.[65] These are, however, not histories of the animals themselves, and are far from histories written from the animals' perspectives.

One exception has drawn my attention. In his article on the Gir lion in the special issue of *History and Theory*, Mahesh Rangarajan[66] argues that although it would be going too far to endow the lions with historical consciousness, they clearly have memories or memory of memories, which, at its simplest level, i.e. for animals, can be measured in terms of adaptive benefit. Rangarajan shows how over the years the lions of Gir in Kathiawar have changed the way they relate to humans. There was a time when the lion was a much sought-after animal by hunters, particularly by princes and kings, as the latter saw it as equal to themselves and a symbol of their royal elitism. Lions were also considered 'dangerous beasts', and as a result of the British policy of elimination of 'dangerous beasts', very few of these big cats were left in this region by 1900. Towards the end of the nineteenth century, the ruler of Junagarh made efforts to protect them by restricting hunting in his own state and the neighbouring regions. After the prolonged drought of 1899–1901, lion attacks on livestock (as well as humans) beyond the forest became commonplace, after which, however, lion-human relations gradually took a turn for the better. After Independence, the Gir Wildlife Sanctuary was created (1965), as the lion was not only a symbol of regional pride, but also became the national animal of the new republic. Lions, living on a mix of domestic livestock—provided to them by villagers (particularly for 'lion shows' to attract tourists) eager to earn revenue—and also wild prey, have thus adapted to human presence and co-inhabit the forest and its neighbourhood in close proximity to resident people. There have been temporary phases of intensifying human-lion conflicts,[67] but on the whole, such conflicts have abated. Gir has developed a pattern of co-existence, though not harmony. Rangarajan suggests that there may have been cross-generational learning among the lions and a sort of evolution (at least in terms of 'lion culture') within a rather short time, i.e. a little more than a century. Human–animal boundaries have thus been renegotiated. Thus, the 'lions of Gir are as much products and actors of a specific history'. In general, big cats in heavily hunted reserves that are now safe havens have lost their fear of jeep-borne observers and are no longer considered that dangerous.

Rangarajan interestingly shows that the conflict in Gir was not just between humans and lions, but also between humans. When the Gir Wildlife Sanctuary was set up, the Maladharis, an old pastoral community of the region, were forcibly resettled as farmers. But some of them—the elderly, outcast and diseased—remained and shared the edges of the Gir forest with lions and leopards, against whom they and their livestock had to fend for themselves. Given the rigid caste system, they had no better alternatives and became 'waste parts' of population. Rangarajan refers to the research of David Quammen[68] who asks, 'Is it inevitable that the cost exacted by alpha predators be borne disproportionately by poor people, while the "haves" can safely enjoy the spiritual and aesthetic pleasure of the Sanctuary's majestic lions?' Indeed, it seems we must understand the historical inequality between humans and animals alongside inequalities among humans themselves; in other words, posthumanism and postcolonialism must go hand in hand.

Another important recent work is Radhika Govindrajan's *Animal Intimacies*.[69] This is not a historical work, strictly speaking, but an anthropological one focused on a cluster of Kumaon villages (primarily the village Pokhri), showing how human and animal lives are intertwined there for better or worse and exploring how these connections produce a sense of relatedness between human and non-human animals. The concept of 'relatedness' seems close to the concept of 'agencement' already discussed. Her basic premise is that one is not formed as a self in isolation but through the 'doing' and 'performing' of relations—both desirable and undesirable. The book mostly confines itself to human perspectives and does not say much on animal perspectives. But the author does try to engage in multispecies ethnography, paying attention to other ways of being, which are related to not just a generalized abstraction called 'animal', but to actual living animals. She recognizes animals' agency, intention and capacity for emotion, and stresses the co-constitution of human and non-human animals as subjects. The spirit of interspecies mutuality and intimacy is beautifully revealed in this work (though not implying an erasure of difference or hierarchy).[70] Govindrajan invokes the works of feminist scholars to question 'natural' categories such as kinship and biology, nature and culture, sex and gender, human and animal, and stresses instead on the particular contexts of their naturalization. She too places her work within the framework of postcolonial scholarship.[71]

In each chapter Govindrajan explores a different form of relatedness. In Kumaon, animals—livestock, cats, dogs—live in intimate proximity to their caregivers, who are mostly women. This involves daily proximity, mutual nurturance and entanglements. Some animals also move between the forest and the village; neither they nor humans are confined to strict boundaries. For example, the leopard living with her cubs on the rocky slope looming over the village, whose call echoes through the village in the evening, announcing her presence in the midst of villagers. There is also the unsettling presence of the 'otherwild' deep inside the forest. There are multiple, shifting human–animal encounters here. Govindrajan studies human–animal encounters in their varied affective relationships, both positive and negative. Moreover, the relations are enacted on an increasingly contested ethical and political terrain, with a range of intervening actors—NGO workers, animal rights activists, Hindu reformers (with regard to cow slaughter in particular). After all, the village today is no longer isolated and self-contained.

The people of Kumaon use kinship terms to describe their relatedness to animals, even the unwanted ones. Knots of connection are not always positive and heartwarming. These may stress difference, exclusion or abuse. For example, the villagers call 'outsider' monkeys Kauravas, undesirable relatives with whom daily battles have to be fought. They do not mind the local monkeys though. Govindrajan also noticed that human relatedness to animals is often inflected by gender. Women relate to animals differently than men. A woman who brought up a *pahari* goat as a family member (indeed, women often draw comparisons between raising children and raising goats) only to sacrifice it to Ma Kalika for her family's good, which caused her terrible grief, nevertheless believed that the goat would understand the need for its own ritual sacrifice in a way that a goat from the plains could not. Indeed, there is a ritual necessity of *jharr* on the part of the goat (i.e. shaking its body) as a sign that the goat consented to his own death. Without it the sacrifice cannot take place. Villagers do not understand the logic of animal rights activists (PFAs) fighting to end 'senseless' cruelty to animals, preaching that one can kill animals for food, but not to appease the gods. The animal rights activists often link their drive with their zeal to reform Hinduism. On the whole, the ethical side of the question of sacrifice becomes very complex.

Particularly complex is the question of cow slaughter, which was banned in 2007 due to the impact of rising Hindu nationalism. But this has only pushed the trade underground, because keeping old cows would be a heavy drain on the villagers' meagre household resources. Hindutvabadis (who teamed up with PFAs) accuse Hindus of all castes rather than Muslims of this illegal trade, and advise them to promote beauty and health products made from cow urine and dung to make old cows viable for the economy. But they fail to capture the complexity of people's relationship with actual cows. Religion is subsumed into politics in a way that does not allow for an examination of questions of affective power and belief. Villagers also consider the cow sacred, but they believe that only *pahari* cows embody divine power, not the crossbred/foreign Jersey cows (born through *sarkari sui* or artificial insemination) that have come to dominate this landscape as a result of an aggressive dairy development programme since 2007. This programme of 'white revolution' along the lines of what the Amul Cooperative had achieved was introduced hand in hand with the ban on cow slaughter. There was a clear anomaly in logic. The logical end of the 'white revolution' is in the slaughter of old cows. Indeed, even Hindutva ideologues know this, hence they urge villagers to use cow urine and dung commercially to make old cows profitable. Strangely, the Hindutvabadis even agree that *desi* cows are superior to Jersey cows, in terms of the quality of milk and in terms of their ritual significance.

On the whole, the Kumaon villagers have a different kind of rationality, deeply rooted in reality. Govindrajan claims that relatedness means varying level of violence, which does not preclude love and care. Relatedness is complicated and is experienced by human and non-human animals alike. For humans, it is locally, culturally imagined. They tend to live an ethical life within this complexity (for Hindu nationalists and their animal rights allies, it is a different ethics, narrow and abstract, where the cow is no more than a metaphor for them). To Govindrajan, relatedness evidently has ethical and political implications. In conclusion, she urges that we should temper our anthropocentric hubris to prevent ecological collapse and make alliances to sustain regenerative life, or in Donna Haraway's words, 'we must make kin'.[72] 'With all its possibilities and perils, relatedness might be all we have.'[73]

But Govindrajan's is a new kind of anthropology. The academic discipline of anthropology is, by definition, anthropocentric; even though, animals have always been important to it. Up to a point, this was largely to come to terms with its origins in colonialism. The assumption that the colonized were closer to nature and animality and that they should remain that way was common to White anthropologists for a long time. However, anthropologists often find humans' relationships with animals—including the meanings assigned to the latter, ways of classifying them, ways of using them and so on—a vantage point from which to investigate human beings and their relationships with one another. Clifford Geertz's famous study of cockfighting in Bali showed how this reflected in the social structure there, as it was really men identifying with their birds. On the other hand, Guggenheim claims that cockfights in the Philippines actually hide and reconstitute the sociocultural process. Bullfighting in Spain has been shown to relate to conflicts over gender and the construction of national and regional identity. Studies of hunting and pastoral practices can also be mentioned in this connection.[74] For example, Anand Pandian studied pastoral relationships between men and animals in a south Indian region shaped by colonialism to understand relationships among humans.[75] Anthropologists have produced interesting works on animals within themes like cultural ecology, domestication, sacrifice, myths, metaphors, etc. There were debates among anthropologists regarding the value of animals from utilitarian perspectives in contrast to their symbolic and structural value.[76] Then came calls to integrate the utilitarian/materialist and intellectualist/symbolic approaches. Whereas the structuralists tend to think that oppositions between nature and culture or humans and animals are fixed, poststructuralists tend to ask questions such as the one posed by Haraway: 'What gets to count as nature, for whom, and at what cost?' Indeed, human–animal boundaries are flexible and people relate to animals in diverse ways. Some anthropologists are trying to get over their inherent anthropocentricism and understand the animals' perspective in the relationship. Nelson, for example, considered the relationship of deer with people as well as people with deer. He defended deer-hunting, though condemned the ways in which deer have been used for scientific research.[77]

Ethical and Methodological Fissures within Animal Studies: Humanism vs. Posthumanism

Ethical and methodological problems still persist within animal studies which include conflicts between humanists and posthumanists.[78] Some scholars want to do away with the subject-centred ethics and politics inherited from Enlightenment (i.e. humanism) and ask the fundamental question of how humans have been separated from animals rather than talk about noble issues like rights. It is argued that championing rights from a safe ontological distance leaving unquestioned the human schema of knowing the subject would change nothing. This is the posthumanist argument.

Animal studies in recent times has been dominated by two paradigms—liberatory hermeneutics (also manifest in feminism, race studies and postcolonialism) and a cultural historicism. Wolfe suggests in his *What is Posthumanism?* that animal studies should eschew both these paradigms and embrace posthumanism, which could fundamentally unsettle the dominant ways of our knowing and thinking. Let us now see how post-humanism claims a distinct place within animal studies.

From Aristotle to Heidegger the problem for humans with regard to animals is that we are so alike and yet so different. Today, however, we are forced to think about species in terms of connection and continuum rather than division and differentiation. Human identity is no longer associated with the abstract mind or soul. The modern era, as Michel Foucault has made us realize, grasps and governs its citizens/subjects at the level of the body. What the feminist scholar O. Oyewumi says in this connection, condemning the entire Western philosophical tradition, is worth quoting:

The much-vaunted Cartesian dualism was only an affirmation of a tradition in which the body was seen as a trap from which any rational person had to escape. Ironically, even as the body remained at the centre of both sociopolitical categories and discourse, many thinkers denied its existence for certain categories of people, most notably themselves…. Women, primitives, Jews, Africans, the poor, and all those who have been considered to be embodied, dominated therefore by instinct and affect, reason being beyond them. They are the Other, and the Other is a body.[79]

This new political relevance of the body in social studies (following its scientific relevance, which we have already discussed) forces us to confront our continuity with other animals. Power acts upon bodies: humans and animals alike are shaped and controlled by modes of biopower.[80] Thus, it seems that a better future for humans and animals can come from critically interrogating the species boundary and rethinking governance and ethics. We have come to realize that human problematizations about non-humans are rarely ever just about non-humans but mediated by other hierarchies of difference. There is a strong urge to explore the connections between speciesism, racism, sexism and other forms of oppression, based on a realization that these logics of domination are intertwined. Agamben and others have pointed out that violence against even human others has often operated through their animalization.[81]

Derrida's arguments in favour of posthumanism are as follows. In his *The Animal That Therefore I Am*[82] he says that all the philosophers who have reflected on animals thought in the form of disavowal which leads to hatred even for human animality; yet, to properly theorize or philosophize this issue we must get over this prejudice. For a long time, capabilities like reason, emotion and language were widely believed to belong to humankind alone, but today, thanks to advanced scientific research, it seems the animal is deprived only of language. Therefore, Derrida argues that we have to deconstruct 'logocentrism' by challenging the idea of human monopoly of language, which should then be followed by challenges to phallogocentrism (a prejudice that privileges the male) and then to carnophallogocentrism (upholding carnivorous sacrifice, vital to our modernity, in the form of violence towards animals). On the other hand, the idea of language should be expanded towards greater inclusivity. Indeed, even before Derrida, Darwin had sought to overcome logocentricism by arguing that touch is a very effective language, an inherited habit that we all share. The language of the eye can be very powerful as well. We have already seen how Erica Fudge (citing Noam Chomsky) refused to consider language as a great divide between humans and non-humans.

In his book, Derrida also evokes the powerful and famous question posed by Bentham about the standing of animals in the eyes of humans: the question is not, can they talk or can they reason, but can they suffer? For Derrida, posing the question in this way 'changes everything'. It addresses inability, vulnerability, passivity and 'non-power at the heart of power'. Instead of recognizing the moral standing of animals because of their agency and the capabilities they share with us, which has been the dominant strategy, most obviously in the animal-rights philosophy of Peter Singer or Tom Regan, Derrida rather draws our attention to our finitude that we share with animals, something that had previously been the mission of humanity to disavow. This is a standard charge levelled against Singer or Regan today, that they are extending a model of human subjectivity to animals, as if they possess our kind of personhood in diminished form. Other important philosophers like Agamben support Derrida. Their arguments do not repudiate humanism, but show how its admirable ambitions are undermined by its conceptual framework.

Derrida notes in this connection that the logic of our political institutions is based on sacrifice, which can take the form of overt killing or letting tens of millions die from hunger and diseases. One of the numerous recent examples, which, of course, was not mentioned by Derrida is the president of Russia waging a war on innocent men, women, and children in Ukraine to maintain the imagined sovereignty and supremacy of his country. Derrida argues that as long as the original separation enacted by the human–animal boundary remains in place, denoting the gap between those who might be killed without any moral or legal consideration and those included within institutions of civil society and ethical community, this sacrifice will continue. It is precisely this structural centrality of the human–animal boundary that requires us to rethink its logic if we wish to contest this ongoing sacrifice which has caused terrible sufferings not only to animals but also to other human beings. From the very beginning of their existence, *Homo sapiens* decided that if some creatures were different from them in terms of appearance or manners and customs, they could be killed with impunity. This is the human schema of knowing and understanding. Animals are, of course, radically different from them; however, *Homo sapiens* massacred even Neanderthals, who were not that much different from them morphologically or culturally. And even within the human order, such otherization has been seen throughout human history with a view to dominate, exploit, and torture. Our conscience is aroused only in regard to those who we consider to be like us, and not in regard to those who we consider 'others'. Recently, a foreign correspondent of an American news channel protested Russia's attack on Ukraine, arguing, 'They are civilized people, they look like us!', which would mean Afghans or Iraqis (who look different) are not worthy of similar compassion.

Derrida argues that it is not our shared ability but rather shared helplessness that should matter. Indeed, according to him, the grounds for sovereignty, on which any right must be based, are the singularity of one's own death (because everyone has to die his/her own death, none other can undergo it). This should help us understand the singularity of all deaths and, thus, to see the other as sovereign and take responsibility for the other as part of one's own community. In this way, animals are placed within the realm of ethical fellow subjects. Humans must accept the responsibility for 'living in general', a responsibility that Derrida argues, is precisely what our philosophical and political traditions seek to avoid in the deployment of the human–animal boundary. He also opines that human claim of sovereignty over animals itself is a groundless claim of the precedence of human over animal life that comes not from observation or logic but from positing in advance a difference that is then tautologically secured by the difference itself—humans have sovereignty, while animals are not sovereign by nature. This, according to Derrida, is utter illogic, sheer stupidity.

Derrida strongly argues that sovereignty is never shaped from above, or on the basis of a decision taken by the victor; it is always shaped from below, by those who are weak, afraid. We humans share our weakness, inability, passivity, embodiment, vulnerability and, eventually death, with animals. We share a common vulnerability to mortality, to social and political power. Of course, as he points out, humans suffer from a second kind of finitude as well—our subjection to the radically 'ahuman technicity' and 'mechanicity of language'; thus, we always easily think of 'our' concepts, 'our' histories. This is, after all, ethnocentrism, on which is based our search for ethical universals supportive of rights philosophy. Hence, Derrida urges us to rethink the humanist schema. Asking the question, 'How to define a human as opposed to animal?', he answers that the only distinctiveness is human bestiality, which a beast is incapable of.

Carey Wolfe, drawing upon Derrida, considers the methodology of animal studies and tries to take it in a new direction[83]—to make a kind of shift that would make it more than another area of socially and ethically responsive cultural studies working to stay abreast of new social movements (in this case, animal rights). He sees animal studies as an academic expression of a big democratic impulse towards greater inclusiveness of every gender, race, sexual orientation, and now, species. Wolfe does not, however, approve of the association of animal studies with cultural studies. For him, animal studies poses a fundamental challenge to the disciplinarity of humanities, including cultural studies, particularly the kind of humanism known as liberalism, which extends the sphere of consideration (intellectual or ethical) to previously marginalized groups without destabilizing the schema of the human who now tends to broaden it through pluralization. Wolfe argues that pluralism here means just incorporation; this is a kind of 'inclusive vagueness' that has allowed much of cultural studies to be appropriated for the ambitious ideology of the exploitative neoliberal order (despite its apparent opposition to the latter). Cultural studies has not been able to break away from the canons of liberal humanism, whose most familiar expression is the rights movements. Extending this kind of pluralism to animal studies and extending the juridical approach of rights to the animal sphere will not suffice, according to Wolfe. Unless we challenge the very basis of our knowledge and the human subject who seeks this knowledge, animal studies would remain trapped in the very humanism and anthropocentrism it sets out to question. It would remain the latest subdisciplinary area of a whole array of academic fields that, since the 1970s, have come to be called 'studies' (gender, race, cultural, film, media, queer). Wolfe argues that even highlighting subjectivity and agency is not enough—it still closes off the human from the animal of animal studies and thus reinstates the human–animal divide in a less visible but more fundamental way, while ostensibly gesturing beyond it. It tacitly assumes the schema of subjectivity to be carried out through critical introspection and self-reflection that is, after all, a hallmark of humanism. This enables the human to recognize the non-human in a gesture of benevolence, characteristic of liberal humanism.

The post-humanist argument thus runs: animal studies should be more invested than any other category of studies in fundamentally rethinking the question of what knowledge is, how knowledge is limited by our 'species-being' (a term made famous by

Karl Marx, though he highlighted its positive aspects). It is precisely here that animal studies intersects with the larger problematic of posthumanism, not in the sense of some fantasy of transcending human embodiment, but in the sense of returning us precisely to the thickness and finitude of human embodiment— our animality, which is unique and different from other forms, but no more different, perhaps, than an orangutan from starfish. Thus, we must also pay serious attention to diversity of animal forms—the human–animal binary is nonsensical. Wolfe says:

Far from surpassing or rejecting the human, [posthumanism] actually enables us to describe the human and its characteristic codes of communication, interaction, meaning, social signification, and affective investment with greater specificity once we have removed meaning from the ontologically closed domain of consciousness, reason, reflection and so on. It forces us to rethink our taken-for-granted human experience(s) … by recontextualizing them in terms of the entire sensorium of other living beings and their own 'autopoietic' ways of being in the world.

Thus, once again, the very term 'animal' is repudiated. Humans have instituted this term to claim the right to dominate non-humans. Derrida, too, thinks that this word is a crime of the first order against animals. Furthermore, the concept 'animal' has a huge political consequence, as it entails a politics of our mindlessly sacrificing them.

However, the basic problem is perhaps that animals studies is always to be undertaken by humans, and that human civilization keeps animals under human control. Our domination over animals has been so normalized and even naturalized over the millenia that it seems very difficult to denormalize and denaturalize it. Thus, even posthumanism can remain the same kind of wishful thinking as humanism. Recently, Gautam Basu Thakur, a critical theorist, argued that even our twenty-first century critical mindscapes have perhaps merely replaced the positive form of Enlightenment anthropocentricism, i.e. 'I am the master of animals' with a more self-consciously negative albeit feel-good form of neoliberal anthropocentricism, i.e. 'I am guilty for mistreating/misrepresenting animals but by admitting this guilt I still am.' 'From subjects who know their superiority over animals, we have today become subjects who know their culpability in the systemic exclusions of animals.'[84] Indeed, scholars like Michael Lundblad call for an end to 'animal studies' and proposes 'animality studies' precisely for this reason. As Lundblad defines it, eschewing '"liking animals", animality studies focuses on discursive constructions of animality in relation to both humans and nonhumans'.[85] This approach is quite popular with postcolonial scholars today, particularly those engaged in literary studies.

But we are not ready to abandon our moral concern for non-human animals so easily despite being aware of its inefficacy, nor are we going to brush aside animal studies as irrelevant. To be optimistic, it can perhaps be argued that animal studies can interrogate the dominating attitude of humans because it is a threshold domain; this threshold may be perceived as a limit but also as enabling renegotiation, as a departure. Wolfe and some other scholars want to make it a mode of departure, what might be called 'critical animal studies'. They urge us to historicize and radicalize both the human and the animal, arguing that neither is a stable and prefabricated being, i.e. that both are effects, and not grounds, of what the humanistic and life sciences count as knowledge, and thus to overcome the covert anthropocentricism associated with the modern Enlightenment thoughts that euphemize violence and uphold the notion of sacrifice.

If overcoming anthropomorphism may always remain a chimera for humans, it seems the best we can do is to problematize the very categories we use to conduct our analysis at the academic level and simultaneously respond to the pragmatic reality of animal sufferings that we find all around us, even if not in the name of the high-sounding political concept of rights. After all, our history shows that it is the predators who enjoy rights over the prey and that humans are the biggest predators on earth. As far as animals are concerned, they are so helpless in the face of human civilization that they cannot even assert rights from their position of weakness, like human rebels sometimes do.

Extending the Ethics of Care to Animals

Approaching the matter at a more practical level, today a number of scholars try to privilege the ethics of care—'Love thy neighbour as thyself'—over the political theory of 'rational citizen' and without stressing the issue of 'rights' too much. These scholars argue that we should nurture a more open-ended conception of the definition of neighbour and ask: Why limit care only to humans? What exactly is it about humans that makes them ethically relevant and excludes non-humans? There is nothing that particularly distinguishes humans from non-humans—'There are no capacities that completely distinguish all humans from all nonhumans. Set the bar too high and you exclude some humans, set it too low and you include lots of nonhumans.' And if one realizes this, one cannot deny the inclusion of non-humans within the sphere of care and concern. Stefan Dolgert, advocates an ethic of care for animals while commenting on an article on care ethic by Barbara Arneil, where he agrees that there may be practical reasons for limiting the scope of concern to certain creatures over others, and for privileging certain relationships over others, but states this is true of any standard ethical or political theory. Parents have more immediate and extensive duties to their children, but that does not lessen the theoretical importance of children's rights as fundamental human rights in general. One might not have the same obligations to wild beasts as to one's mother or one's dog, but that should not belittle the consideration for those spatially (and emotionally) distant creatures. Humans and non-humans are equal citizens in the biotic community.[86]

The ethics of care is based on interdependence theory. None of us is, wholly or partially independent of the care of others. Thinking rationally, the theory of interdependence begs the question of species border and urges us to include non-humans within its sphere.[87] Dolgert asserts that if animals are excluded at the outset, that would upset the very venture of interdependence. Exclusion of animals from the sphere of interdependence is grounded in theories of difference.

There is usually tension between the conception of interdependence and the valuing of difference. Stressing the 'inter' in inter-dependence may lead to a devaluing of a given creature or a species in the web of life or of a human who may depend on someone else but may not be depended on himself. There are many people considered second-class citizens in human society, for example disabled persons. Non-humans are seen as all the more disabled—'less than humans'. Dolgert argues that we have to flesh out the difference aspects of interdependence to overcome this problem. His suggestion is as follows: let us not see disability (as well as being non-human) as a tragedy, deficit or abnormality. Each creature, whether a normal or a disabled human or an 'abled' dog, possesses a unique perspective on the mystery of life, which is to some extent inaccessible to any other being. Everyone, from this vantage point, is similarly abled and disabled in relation to everyone else. All creatures, great and small, are co-perceivers in a world whose macrocosm is inseparable from, indeed composed of, microcosms of perception that each being inhabits. Therefore, each being is epistemologically, experientially and bodily interdependent upon the teeming multitude of other beings for an understanding and fulfillment of life. This should lead to an appreciation for other forms of life, disabled humans or abled non-humans. It must be noted that Dolgert's arguments are different from those of Peter Singer, who argues in favour of animals from a utilitarian point of view: if an animal's use-value is based on its capacities, such as communication through language, then people with linguistic limitations, e.g. children or speech-retarded people, may be experimented upon in laboratories; if their lack of such capacities entitle us to eat them, then why not use children for this purpose? Unlike Singer, Dolgert actually seeks to expand upon rather than undermine the rights of disabled humans.

Utilitarian philosophy may indeed complicate this matter. It is, after all, the utilitarian approach that has led to human aggression on animals. Now, it can easily lead to a choice between variously disabled humans and abled non-humans by pitting one against another. Gary L. Francione in *Animals as Persons: Essays on the Abolition of Animal Exploitation*,[88] demands a radical change in the legal and moral status of non-human animals, arguing in favour of a principle of equal consideration for all. He uses Tom Regan's hypothetical example in this attempt: five survivors including a dog are sharing a lifeboat made for four, and so one has to be thrown overboard. Regan decides that we as humans are morally obliged to kill the dog. Francione, however, asks whether it would not be difficult to reach this decision if the dog as well as the four men were extraordinarily gifted and a fifth man there was an average working-class adult (an ordinary man considered to be somewhat diminutive and, hence, 'disabled' on the scale of human existence). Francione takes an uncompromising stand while upholding animal protectionism and advocates veganism as a practical solution. He also asserts that animals cannot be considered property and wants legal protection for them, similar to that enjoyed by humans.

But even 'ethics of care' may not be able to ensure the good of all animals. As Barbara Arneil, in her reply to Dolgert argues,[89] if the theory of interdependence rests on two basic principles, 'dependence' and 'independence', looking at it through the lens of 'dependence' may make us feel obliged to take care of animals. But this may only be a qualified obligation. She points out that though on the one hand it has been argued by proponents of care ethics that domestic animals under human care should be treated well,[90] there are some scholars who assert that this should include a provision that humans may ethically 'conceive animals … as food'.[91] With respect to the second principle, i.e. 'independence', Arneil dismisses animals' claim to independence out of hand. According to her, only humans have aspiration to independence and non-humans do not. She claims that this is a basic distinction between humans and non-humans and hence between disabled humans and abled non-humans as well. She says in defense of her argument, 'Pets do not seek independence'. This can of course be opposed with the argument that left to themselves most animals would lead an independent life. We know for sure that many of them are fiercely independent, both individually and in terms of their species as a whole.[92]

Indeed, an ethic of care is likely to have many limitations. Sometimes, we have 'care and use' policies for experimental animals. Accordingly, laws pay attention to habitat conditions, pain control, euthanasia protocols, etc., in this regard, affirming that these animals as sentient, conscious and morally significant subjects. But we have already seen that this is a discourse of welfare that has many limitations, ambivalence and exclusions. It erases biological facts like pain by legal decree, wherein life becomes subject to a procedural regime, which is the realm of Foucault's biopower where self-aggrandizing imperatives rather than political or cultural rationality dominates or Agamben's 'sovereign power' which is both inside the law (the final arbiter) and outside it (as a force deciding the limit as well as the purview of judgment).[93] Indeed, Francione argues that improving the use and treatment of animals is a deceitful idea, because it accepts the premise that animals can and should be used in the first place (though presenting this argument in the form of a rights discourse might not be effective).

Many would, of course, find Francione's arguments unacceptable for an entirely opposite reason. They would consider it an extreme stand in favour of animals and against humans. On the other hand, for those who promote violent direct action in the name of animal liberation, it may not be extreme enough. There is a strange pattern of human attitudes toward other living beings, human or non-human, in that helping one necessitates heartlessly condemning the other to destruction. Singer is often condemned by disability rights activists as a force of evil. In nineteenth-century England, animal welfare issues were seen as a contest between working-class people and animals. Similar problems were witnessed in nineteenth- and twentieth-century Bengal. The infamous Marichjhanpi incident is a case in point. On the one hand urban, middle-class people romanticize rural people/indigenous communities as having a more 'authentic' relationship with animals and, on the other hand, they looked away when the police fired on the people of Marichjhanpi in the Sundarbans to reserve the area as an abode for tigers. More recently in India, concern for cows has led to killing of human beings on the suspicion that the latter have consumed cow meat (which was later proven to be an incorrect assumption). Needless to say, the humans who commit such crimes against humanity do not much care for the well-being of cows. Animal issues remain highly contentious, with people taking sides according to their respective predilections.

Individualizing Animals as a Method of Empathy

I believe that the most effective method of ensuring animals' well-being, which has emerged from the field of animal studies, is to view them as individuals. Thierry Hoquet in his article 'Animal Individuals: A Plea for a Nominalistic Turn in Animal Studies' makes a case for animal individuals.[94] He argues that 'animals', a catch-all category, denies individuality to non-human animals (although, perhaps we can say the same for different human categories as well, such as peasants, Muslims, etc.) and that individuality implies a dimension of existential singularity as well as a political and legal claim of emancipation. We already know how some scholars are trying to focus on individual humans and even individual animals by extending their methods (though perhaps my own discipline, history, is not yet adept in dealing with individual humans, leave aside individual animals). The claim of subjecthood and agency of animals that we have already discussed also rests on their individualization. Biologists too are increasingly concerned with individuals. They question standard norms of behaviour and preferences and even physical characteristics in particular species. Hoquet's paper defies Aristotle's claim that there is a science inasmuch as there is a generality and shows how biological science is overcoming its obsession with generality. Thus, the relevance of animal individuals is no longer just a philosophical issue led by postmodern scholars.

Biologists are trying to address animal individuals in their methodology. We have already noted how researchers of animal behaviour and conservationists are capturing their singularity. This seems to be necessary even to have an accurate census of the animal population, For example, pug marks are considered equivalent to human fingerprints for a proper system of identification; elephants are being individualized based on the different parts of their body—the shape of their trunk, the edge of their ear; and zebras are individualized by the unique layout of their stripes. We may also point out different temperaments and behaviours, colour preference etc., which not only widely vary but can even be idiosyncratic.

This individuality is not contradictory to generality. It makes sense only in relation to some general concepts; hence, focusing on animal individuals does not entail departing from the Aristotelian dictum that there is only knowledge of the general. But at the same time, an animal individual is not just a token or a type. Each one has its distinct personalities, interests, emotions, behaviours, etc. As Fudge says, there is no such thing as the cow, there are only individual cows.[95] Thus, essentialism regarding animals is to be avoided, just as in the case of mankind. Consequently, if one treats an animal as an individual, one cannot easily brutalize it. Even Descartes cared for his own dog whom he called 'Monsieur Grat', thus individualizing him. Needless to say, the emphasis on individuality has considerable ethical consequences and claims 'dignity and freedom for each'. It is in this way that non-human animals are becoming persons in the human, moral and even legal sense. Animals are being provided for in their owners/masters' wills. Francione too claims animal rights at both the philosophical and legal levels on the basis of recognition of the individuality and uniqueness of each animal.

Suggesting that animals are, like us, individual subjects, may, however, run the risk of anthropomorphism. But it has been argued that if anthropomorphism helps us develop empathy rather than set us apart, then perhaps it is a good thing. As Frans de Waal (whose work on chimpanzees is well-known) argues, anthropo-denial—a denial of human-like characteristics to animals and animal-like characteristics to humans—is far more pernicious than anthropomorphism. We can perhaps extend our creative imagination to understand animals through anthropomorphism. They are different, of course. But differences exist even among humans. We may never adequately translate how a subject or subjects different from us feel, think or act. This is a problem for any ethnographer, historian or any other practitioner of human studies. However, today we want to believe that differences not only separate, they also connect. As Radhika Govindrajan suggests, perhaps what we need is 'open anrhopomorphism'. She says that this is a risk worth taking 'in the interest of following the trail of the qualitative and the subjective in animal life, and of creativity in nature...'. At the same time, perhaps 'we might move beyond anthropomorphism as regards ourselves: our inveterate vanity regarding our assumed species identity, based on the specious grounds of our sole proprietorship of language, thought and creativity'.[96] Govindrajan shows that this kind of empathy may emerge out of caregiving to an individual animal. In Kumaon, where she carried out her field study, women act as caregivers to animals, Thus, as Govindrajan notes, women usually relate to animals more closely than men. Caregiving is not just gendered, it is also inter-corporeal; for example, in the case of a woman, whom Govindrajan calls 'Bimla Chachi', who had once helped a female goat give birth. Bimala Chachi told Govindrajan that the kid considered her its 'second mother'. Here, Govindrajan's comments:

While the kid who followed Bimla chachi around might not exactly have thought her as a 'second mother'—the term chachi used—she certainly seemed to recognize in her what Donna Haraway terms 'the presence of a significant other', someone whom she could play with and love, someone that she could trust to take care of her.[97]

Maybe it is just animal instinct, but for humans too love is largely instinctual.

If we consider pet-keeping the trait that epitomizes individualization and anthropomorphization of animals (as well as loving and being loved by them), we can perhaps find some corroboration of what Govindrajan says in biological science. It is true that pet-keeping is largely culturally determined and cross-cultural patterns of pet-keeping vary. But biologists tell us that it is culture combined with a sort of predisposition, exemplifying the type of gene-culture interactions that shape many other aspects of human behaviour (we can perhaps draw a parallel with marriage: the mutual attraction of a man and a woman and their pair-bonding is a predisposition, but choice of partner depends on culture). Some researchers argue that pet-keeping is a by-product of evolved tendencies linked to the care of human offspring. There is neurophysiological and behavioural evidence that humans are naturally attracted to creatures with infantile facial characteristics like big eyes, large crania and soft, round facial features. Anthropomorphism, the tendency to project human mental states onto non-human species, too, appears to be a deeply rooted aspect of human cognition. The degree to which people can anthropomorphize and empathize with animals is affected by culture as well as what is termed 'biophilia' by the sociobiologist E.O. Wilson. He defined it as an 'innate tendency of focus on life and life-like process'(1984), but did not claim that this is a hard-wired human trait. In fact, he later moderated his view and wrote, 'Biophilia is not a single instinct but a complex of learning rules that can be teased apart and analyzed individually.' Thus, while a tension between cultural and biological explanations of pet-keeping remains, even those who are inclined to explain it in cultural terms cannot deny that to some extent it is an innate facet of human nature. Harold Herzog, for example, says that we are among the most social of species and our attachments to other species are rooted in neuro-hormonal mechanisms that have evolved to facilitate social relationships with other humans. Studies have found that interacting with pets stimulate the release of oxytocin, a hormone that promotes social bonding. Oxytocin is known as the hormone of love.[98]

Hence, loving an animal is within human nature, facilitated by the former's individualization and anthropomorphization. But humans are complex beings; and paradoxically, individualization and anthropomorphization can have an opposite effect as well. Evolutionary theorists tell us that anthropomorphism first evolved in *Homo sapiens* 40,000 years ago. A hunter who could project himself into the mind of his prey would be more successful. On the other hand, the same ability made early hunters empathize with the animals they were trying to kill (hence, they designed rituals to alleviate the sense of guilt for killing a fellow creature).

Call for Love

The fact is, human beings encompass both love and cruelty in their nature. For love to triumph over cruelty, a special 'civilizational drive' is needed.[99] Govindarajan reminds us that we need to cultivate love, and that love is not restricted to humans only. Perhaps it is anthropomorphic to say that animals also love, that they want to live in sync with other beings. But this degree of anthropomorphism is perhaps permissible for the sake of understanding animals and for improving human–animal relationships.

However, as Govindrajan reminds us, love may not be entirely selfless; it may even endorse cruelty. A woman who brings up a goat or a cow ultimately endorses its sacrifice or hands it to the butcher.[100] Love, at least in the sense of long-term attachment(as in pet-keeping), is nurtured in the minds of individuals *for* individuals. For someone to love all humans or all members of another species with equal intensity is not possible. Even if we delimit the meaning of love and think of compassion—concern and care out of empathy and sympathy, particularly a painful feeling for someone's helplessness and sufferings—how broad can the scope of its expression be? How much compassion can one afford to show? It is a fundamental problem that life needs to live off the living and so there is an inherent competition in nature for survival. This generates a tension between some creatures' will-to-live and their willingness to negate the life that others live. How do we reconcile this tension? Throughout history, humans have mostly argued that animals are forms of life without ethical significance. Thus, how can one hope to change things?

It seems that just evoking love is too simplistic a solution. The answer perhaps lies in a more holistic understanding of our complex interdependence, material and mental, with other creatures, and in developing a reverence for all lives. This is what Govindrajan has called 'relatedness'. This sense of relatedness with animals rests primarily on finding similarities with them and understanding that we share with them our embodied existence with all its joy and vulnerability. One remembers in this connection Albert Schweitzer, a theologian, philosopher and physician (and a Nobel Peace Prize winner), whose concern for animals was grounded in the notion of 'reverence for life', which came from the realization of a simple truth:

In everything you recognize yourself again. The beetle that lies dead in your path—it was something that lives, that struggled for its existence like you, that rejoiced in the sun like you, that knew anxiety and pain like you. And now it is nothing more than decomposing material—as you, too, shall be sooner or later.[101]

Schweitzer claimed that in this realization 'the dissimilarity, the strangeness, between us and other creatures is . . . removed'. Reverence for life mandates empathy and compassion for non-human animals. Humans are expected to devote the same level of fervency they have for their own lives to every other human; but, as Schweitzer asserts, for the truly ethical person, it cannot end here and must be extended to non-humans.

Schweitzer's view is anthropocentric in that he regards human beings as the only creatures who could transcend the law of nature. According to him, humans have the spiritual capacity to overcome the reality of nature, for they can turn their 'will-to-live' into a 'will-to-love' and into a sense of moral responsibility to protect other creatures (thus giving the word 'love' a very broad connotation). But, of course, he recognized that humans suffer from a tension too in this respect. However, for him, any kind of harming of animals other than out of absolute necessity was abhorrent. The spiritualist aspect of the argument of Schweitzer, a religiously inclined man, may seem obscurantist. But perhaps we can translate it into Marx's idea of 'human essence' or 'species being' which must logically extend to non-humans too. This idea points to the 'radical need' of every human individual to be at one with the universal—by overcoming 'alienation from oneself, from society and from nature which includes animals, and by discovering human relationship underlying utilitarian/commodity relationship'. Those Marxists who emphasize the 'humanitarian' aspect of Marx's teachings claim that only in this way can humans return to their essential state of being. According to some Western Marxists, this is the dynamics operating in everyday life and within human beings themselves, for a fundamental change of the existing order.[102] In my view, this also upholds the idea of man's moral responsibility towards animals. As animals cannot protest or assert their rights, this leaves humans with the responsibility to do so on their behalf.[103]

This also foregrounds animals' difference from humans. They are different as they cannot speak. As Susan D. Jones, a prominent animal historian, says, 'animals are perpetual "others", doomed to have their interests represented to humans by other humans'.[104] But as we have pointed out, differences not only separate, they can also connect. Indeed, in the case of individual love, it is said that opposites attract. Looking at this issue more broadly, this sense of difference may be vested with a moral significance, as was asserted by a Gandhi. We will try to understand Gandhi's standpoint in the final section of this chapter.

Is Indian Thought Regarding Animals Different?

It is often said that Oriental traditions have a different attitude to animals. The examples of Taoism (as opposed to Confucianism), Hinduism, Jainism and Buddhism are commonly cited in this connection. All these creeds lay emphasis on the fact that man is a part of nature and has no right to dominate over nature, including animals. It is argued that Hinduism has a strong ecological sensibility, which is based on the idea that man is not separate from the animal world and that we are all integral parts of an organic whole. Moreover, it is one's action or karma that determines whether men and animals go up or down in the cycle of rebirth, until they achieve moksha or liberation. The Vedas, Upanishads, the epics all stressed this intimate relationship between humans and non-humans. Wendy Doniger argues that the term ahimsa or non-violence in the Vedas originally applied not to relationships among humans alone, but to relationships between humans and animals.[105] Our epics describe stories like that of King Sibi, who gave protection to a pigeon that was under attack by a hawk and was even ready to give up his own life for the sake of the bird.

Some animals were deified in the Hindu tradition. The cow was considered sacred in Vedic hymns. Monkeys were considered divine as they were faithful followers of the god Rama. Lions were associated with the goddess Durga. Similarly there were other animals associated with other gods and goddesses. But Vedic thought was caught between espousing ahimsa and performing animal sacrifice. Classical Hinduism too was not a safe haven for non-humans. They were perceived as lower forms of life. Unlike in Christianity, however, this was not because animals did not possess soul/atman. The key distinction, as Lance Nelson points out, was cognitive, moral and ritual—only humans are able to receive and absorb revelation from the Vedas, that is, only humans have access to dharma. Animals are ignorant, unintelligent, unable to reason, violent and so on. Despite their possession of atman, they are dominated by *tamas* (darkness).[106] The notion of transmigration or rebirth allows for the same soul to be born as either a human or an animal, but an animal rebirth is regarded as a punishment. Thus, the Hindu perception of animals hinged on a strange paradox. Furthermore, for a Hindu, the idea of inferiority of animals was reinforced by religious and ritualistic concepts of impurity associated with most animals. It was also closely tied to the notions of social hierarchy and marginalization of low castes. Cows considered to be sacred were associated with the brahmins, whereas dogs stigmatized as impure were connected to Chandals or outcastes.[107] Such complex attitudes supporting race, caste and species distinctions continues into modern times.

Attitudes towards animals in the Indian subcontinent were neither constant nor monolithic, but shifting as well as complex. Ahimsa as a practice was not always carried out. The ideal of ahimsa developed fully only with the rise of Buddhism and Jainism, both of which involved a reverence for life. There are stories from the Buddha's boyhood describing him saving a swan that had been shot by his cousin Devadatta. The Jatakas, tales of the previous and future births of the Buddha, depict him in both human and animal forms. On the whole, an ambivalence regarding treatment of animals has always existed, but a systematic and comprehensive history of Indian thoughts in regard to animals is yet to be written.

Samiparna Samanta has, however, written about the Bengali bhadralok's thinking with regard to animals in nineteenth-century Bengal. Some were champions of animal protection, for example Peary Chand Mitra who was a member of the SPCA. But this protectionist attitude did not rest on a simple moral ground. The bhadralok, in the age of incipient nationalism, claimed kindness as part of the glorious national, specifically Vedic, tradition. The British, however, challenged this concept of Vedic ahimsa by emphasizing an innate Indian cruelty. There emerged a debate concerning vegetarianism and animal cruelty, with each player attempting to associate its own culture with an inherent kindness. As Samanta shows, the Bengali Hindu middle class tended to combine Vedic ahimsa with epidemiology and a stress on science; gradually science became more important to them.[108] From the mid-nineteenth century, meat-eating was regarded as responsible for the 'manliness' of Europeans. Doctors recommended eating fish and meat in the name of science. It was also argued that cruel handling of animals to be slaughtered rendered the flesh unwholesome, which made the conditions of slaughterhouses a major issue. The stress on meat-eating that had developed among the bhadralok from the mid-nineteenth century to counter the charges of effeminacy hurled at them by the British masters, however, shifted by the beginning of the twentieth. Now there was an emphasis on vegetarianism. But it was not just an evocation of the ethical arguments of Vaishnavism or Jainism. Vegetarianism was seen as healthy, able to prevent all diseases. The widespread outbreak of cattle murrain was likely one reason behind this new attitude. As early as 1858, Akshay Kumar Dutta, who is considered a pioneer of modern scientific thinking in Bengal, countered the doctors who advocated meat-eating. He put forward both ethical and scientific arguments for this, claiming meat-eating was against not only Hindu dharma, but also human *prabritti* (natural inclination). He also argued that vegetarianism made one physically stronger. Even Mir Mosharaff Hossain, a member of the Muslim gentry, condemned cow-killing in his *Go-Jiban*, drawing from both the Hindu Shastras and the Koran. Nirendranath Basu argued that animal slaughter awakened animal instincts in men and he blamed this for the outbreak of the First World War. To the nationalists, meat-eating/vegetarianism became markers of the civilizational character of a nation, and they equated this binary with the material West/spiritual East. Ramendrasundar Tribedi, who like Akshay Dutta is known as a pioneer of scientific thinking in Bengal, however, had a different take on the matter of meat-eating. He opined that the natural inclination of humans was towards meat-eating. However, he also argued that it was cruel and anti-religious (adharma) to eat meat and noted with the predictable nationalist pride that the ideal of ahimsa originated in India and not in Europe. He hoped that one day humans, with the aid of science, would be strong enough to not be cruel to non-humans and not consume meat anymore. On the whole, the bhadralok showed considerable ambivalence regarding the matter.[109]

In the modern period, one Indian who initially derived his idea of non-violence towards non-humans from Jainism and Vaishnava Hinudism is Gandhi.[110] This led him to include not only all humanity (including the British, in the context of the national movement) within the boundaries of ahimsa, but also non-humans. He was against religious sacrifice of animals as well as scientific experiments on them. He chose vegetarianism as part of his personal truth and passion, and he was dangerously sincere about it. When his son was suffering from typhoid, which had no cure then, the only thing the doctor recommended was meat soup. However, Gandhi refused to follow this prescription because, as he said, he was unable to take a life for the life of his son. Gandhi also sought to preach vegetarianism publicly. In the beginning, this inclination was more due to religious and family influences, but gradually he grounded his ahimsa in more coherent reason and ethics, thus expanding his rationale for its practice. Invoking tradition was not enough for him. Indeed, for him true principles of morality stood outside history and tradition. Regarding the warrant for animal sacrifice in the Shastras he said, 'Some will retort that there is warrant for vivisection in Ayurveda. If there is, I am sorry. No warrant even in the four Vedas can sanctify sacrilege.' He studied a variety of modern writers' works on vegetarianism and commented, 'Ethically they had arrived at the conclusion that man's supremacy over the lower animals meant not that the former should prey upon the latter, but that the higher should protect the lower.'

Gandhi's extension of ahimsa to animals was

based on his moral perception of man and was hence anthropocentric, just as in the case of Schweitzer. But while Schweitzer's emphasis was on similarities, Gandhi's thought rested rather on the idea of differences and hierarchy. Man held a higher place than non-human animals in his cosmic ethics. It was the animal's ability to suffer that formed his foundation of *ahimsa* (as in the case of Derrida, but of course with a different argument, with Derrida stressing on similarity and Gandhi on difference). Humanity's greatness did not derive from their ability to utilize the 'lower creation' to its benefit. On the contrary, human greatness rested in the ability to rise above nature's bloody competition and to compassionately care for lesser creatures. 'Man's destiny is to replace the law of the jungle with the law of conscious love', he said. In his outlook, man had a sense of deep moral responsibility as the greatest creature of all creation. Thus, Gandhi's ahimsa encompassed not just refraining from eating meat, but positive activism as well. While he supported the cow-protection movement, at the same time he wanted to ensure the welfare of all animals: 'He is a poor specimen of Hinduism who stops merely at cow-protection when he can extend the arm of protection to other animals. The cow merely stands as a symbol, and protection of the cow is the least he is expected to undertake.'

However, Gandhi also had utilitarian concerns and would sometimes permit killing of animals as a necessary evil; for example, when monkeys became a menace to the well-being of man. But he would not permit killing of another human on this ground: 'It cannot be because, however bad, they are as we are.'

He justified this discrimination in terms of man's faculty of reason, which, according to him, monkeys did not have. This is an idea of essential human-non-human difference and asserts the former's superiority and the latter's inferiority (which, though, does not conform to Cartesian logic, and does not deny a non-human the right to live). However, for Gandhi, even necessary violence called for contrition. He recognized the limitations set on ahimsa by the nature of the world and regretted that man's non-violence had not reached the stage of perfection where this could be fully avoided. But the scope of 'necessary violence' was surely very limited for Gandhi, who believed that 'the world has enough for everyone's need, not for everyone's greed'. So the 'wet markets' like that of Wuhan that helped transmit the deadly Corona virus all over the globe threatening the very existence of mankind would not have been 'needed' in his scheme of things.

The world of humans on the whole has always remained confused and deceitful regarding its attitude to animals. It seems that the human society of the East is not very different from its western counterpart in this regard, though perhaps some cultural differences can be noticed. Despite the so-called Eastern 'traditions', i.e. philosophical and literary inspirations to human compassion, indifference and cruelty continue to dominate our reality. Indeed, it seems whatever progress in the direction of humanitarian treatment of animals has been achieved in the West is far from being realized in India. For example, in the West, slaughterhouses and meat-packing plants have been moved to the outskirts of cities, if not outside of them altogether (though, of course, few people want to know about what goes on in them). Here, the butchering is done before our eyes, and we often prefer it too, just to be sure that we are getting the best-quality meat. Some humans even get a sadistic pleasure out of this.

I wrote this book when humankind was experiencing the peak of the Covid-19 epidemic and there were lockdowns everywhere. There was news that slaughterhouses were shutting down in America due to widespread infection among workers, leading to culling of thousands of farm animals by suffocation (shutting down the ventilator system of pig barns with the addition of CO_2, thus essentially cooking them alive), 'blunt force trauma' (slamming piglets against the ground) and suchlike methods that animal welfare groups deemed 'inhumane'.[111] We humans increase the populations of animals for utilitarian purposes, and then kill them mercilessly when we cannot use them. Human beings do not seem to have changed much as a result of the epidemic. Thus, the question I raised at the end of my 'Prologue' has yet to receive a positive answer: 'Will the post-Corona world be a better place for all humans and animals?' Human beings have not been introspecting and envisioning a compassionate world by looking at the world through the lens of the Covid-19 pandemic. We still believe in unlimited progress by establishing human supremacy over nature, consuming more than what we need just for the sake of consumption, and hurting countless humans and animals for this purpose. Will our civilization redefine itself? Will we ever abandon our selfishness and accept the responsibility for 'living in general', i.e. living for others? It is only then that human–animal relationships will change for the better!

Notes

1.   Ryan Gunderson, 'The First-generation Frankfurt School on the Animal Question: Foundations for a Normative Sociological Animal Studies', *Sociological Perspectives*, vol. 57, no. 3, 2014.

2.   Max Horkheimer, *Dawn and Decline: Notes, 1926–1931 and 1950–1969*, New York: Seabury Press, 1978.

3.   Max Horkheimer and Theodor W. Adorno, *Dialectic of Enlightenment: Philosophical Fragments*, 1947 repr. in English, Stanford: Stanford University Press, 1969.

4.   See Sarah E. McFarland, 'The "Animal" is a Verb: Liberating the Subject of Animal Studies', *JAC*, vol. 30, nos. 3–4, 2010.

5.   Brett Walker, 'Animals and the Intimacy of History', *History and Theory*, vol. 52, no. 4, 2013, p. 55. We are going to refer to this journal extensively in this chapter.

6.   This is what Antonio Damasio, Professor of Neuroscience, Psychology and Philosophy and Director of the Brain and Creativity Institute at the University of Southern California, says emphatically in his book *The Strange Order of Things: Life, Feeling, and the Making of Cultures*, New York: Pantheon Books, 2018.

7.   Yuval Noah Harari, *Sapiens: A Brief History of Humankind*, UK: Penguin Random House, 2011.

8.   Ibid.

9.   Alfred W. Crosby, *Ecological Imperialism: The Biological Expansion of Europe, 900–1900*, New York: Cambridge University Press, 1986.

10. The evolving human–animal relationship in Western history with special reference to England has been presented by Brian Fagan, *The Intimate Bond: How Animals Shaped Human History*, New York, London: Bloomsbury, 2015. One may also look at Linda Kalof, *Looking at Animals in Human History*, London: Reaktion Books, 2007, which is about visual and textual representations of animals and how this has been changing with changing social conditions. See Karl Steel, *How to Make a Human: Animals and Violence in Middle Ages*, Columbus: Ohio State University Press, 2011; Katherine Kate, *A Cultural History of Animals in the Age of Empire*, New York: Berg Publishers, 2007.

11. Emile Durkheim, cited in Dipesh Chakrabarty, *The Climate of History in a Planetary Age*, New Delhi: Primus Books, 2021.

12. Harriet Ritvo, *The Animal Estate: The English and Other Creatures in Victorian England*, Cambridge, MA: Harvard University Press, 1989.

13. Teresa Magnum, 'Animal Angst: Victorians Memorialize their Pet', in *Victorian Animal Dreams: Representations of Animals in Victorian Literature and Culture*, ed. Deborah Denenholz Morse and Martin A. Danhay, Farnham, Surrey: Ashgate, 2007.

14. Martin A. Danahay, 'Nature Red in Hoof and Paw: Domestic Animals and Violence in Victorian Art', in *Victorian Animal Dreams: Representations of Animals in Victorian Literature and Culture*, ed. Deborah Denenholz Morse and Martin A. Danhay, Farnham, Surrey: Ashgate, 2007.

15. Maneesha Deckha, 'Welfarist and Imperial: The Contributions of Anticruelty Laws to Civilizational Discourse', *American Quarterly*, vol. 65, no. 3, 2013. Deckha's argument focuses on the imperial underpinning of welfare laws for animals.

16. Keith Thomas, *Man and the Natural World: Changing attitudes in England, 1500–1800*, UK: Allen Lane, 1983.
17. However, Steintrager has critiqued Thomas, arguing that during Enlightenment there was a major transition in human understanding of 'humanity' and 'cruelty' as it was now believed that humans feel pity more than other creatures because they are reasonable, that it was reason that activated and enabled compassion. It was because reason was prioritized over compassion in this respect that a boundary was drawn between 'legitimate' and 'illegitimate' cruelty. James A. Steintrager, *Cruel Delight: Enlightenment Culture and the Inhuman*, Bloomington: Indiana University Press, 2004. See also Samiparna Samanta, 'Cruelty Contested: The British, Bengalis, and Animals in Colonial Bengal, 1850–1920', PhD thesis, Florida State University, 2012, p. 31, which has drawn my attention to this critique.
18. Harold A. Herzog, 'Biology, Culture, and Origins of Pet-Keeping', *Animal Behaviour and Cognition*, New York: Sciknow Publications Ltd., 2014.
19. Carla Nappi, 'On Yeti and Being Just: Carving the Borders of Humanity in Early Modern China', in *Animals and Human Imagination: A Companion to Animal Studies*, ed. Aaron Gross and Anne Vallely, New York: Columbia University Press, 2012. She draws on a sixteenth-century compendium of *materia medica* by Li Shizhen, considered the father of modern science and medicine in China, to draw readers into lively debates over the limits of being human. Li also tried to understand the concept of trans-species metamorphosis, e.g. when a human becomes a beast upon eating human flesh. Who or what could be legitimately defined as 'food' also became a focus in the construction of a boundary

over the traditional practices of consuming human body parts (hair, urine, flesh etc.).

20. Samanta, 'Cruelty Contested', p. 37.

21. See Shafqat Hussain, 'Forms of Predation: Tiger and Markhor Hunting in Colonial Governance', *Modern Asian Studies*, vol. 46, no. 5, 2012. He compares the late nineteenth and early twentieth-century sport of hunting *markhor*, a mountain goat, by the British in the frontier region of Kashmir, with their hunting of tigers, particularly man-eating ones, in the subcontinent. Through this comparison he shows two competing visions of colonial governance. In the tiger's case, they suspended conventional hunting codes, justifying this with their motive to protect Indian society from 'wild' nature. In the *makhor*'s case, they used *begar*/forced labour, which they justified by claiming that it was a civilization-less area where a coercive form of government was needed. The effort to keep nature from penetrating culture and to push culture to penetrate nature—these were the two modes of colonial governance, not necessarily opposed to one another. In the *makhor*'s case, tribal people were seen as part of nature, and in the tiger's case, the farmers seemed closer to a civilized state. Also see Shafqat Hussain, 'Sport-hunting, Fairness and Colonial Identity Collaboration and Subversion in the Northwestern Frontier Region of the British Empire', *Conservation and Society*, vol. 8, no. 2, 2010, where he shows how the idea of fairness in indigenous hunting practices often clashed with the 'moral ecology' of the colonial hunters. In the late nineteenth century, the British passed game laws to limit hunting by colonial officers and sports hunters, rendering hunting by natives illegal or out of reach (by setting high license fees), even though the British had to depend on the latter's cooperation for hunting. The

population of many game animals suffered from the brutal onslaught at the hands of British sportsmen.

22. Also see Pratik Chakrabarti, 'Beasts of Burden: Animals and Laboratory Research in Colonial India', *History of Science*, vol. 48, no. 2, 2010, p. 125.

23. *Report of the Calcutta Society for Cruelty to Animals for the Year 1861*, National Library, Kolkata, cited by Samanta in her dissertation 'Cruelty Contested', p. 9.

24. Samanta, 'Cruelty Contested'. Also see her article 'Cattle, Cruelty, Cow Doctors: Examining Animal Health in Rural Bengal, 1850–1920', in *Tilling the Land: Agricultural Knowledge and Practices in Colonial India*, ed. Deepak Kumar and Bipasha Raha, Delhi: Primus Books, 2016.

25. An article that helped me form some preliminary ideas about this is Koyeli Chakravorti and Madhumita Chatterjee, 'History of Speciesist Thought', *History*, 2002. An important book is W.E.H. Lecky, *History of European Morals from Augustus to Charlemagne*, London: Longmans, 1869. Also see Sharon Sliwinski, 'The Gaze Called Animal: Notes for a Study on Thinking', in *Selected Works of Sharon Sliwinski*, Canada: Western University, 2011. *History and Theory*, vol. 52, no. 4, 2013, has also helped me in further understanding Western thought regarding animals.

26. Indeed, research scientists have been pointing out that inter-species variability in genetic, physiological and biochemical terms is too high to draw parallels, that the importance of animals in medical/scientific research has been overstated, and that medicines tested on animals often produce harmful results for humans.

27. For example, Thomas Willis, *Two Discourses Concerning the Soul of Brutes*, London: Thomas Dring, 1672.

28. Peter Singer, *Animal Liberation*, New York: Avon Books, 1975; Tom Regan, *The Case for Animal Rights*, Berkeley: University of California Press, 1983. Also see David DeGrazia, *Animal Rights: A Very Short Introduction*, Oxford: Oxford University Press, 2002; Alison Hills, *Do Animals have Rights?*, UK: Icon Books, 2005.

29. Cary Wolfe's article '"Human, All Too Human": Animal Studies and Humanities', *Publication of the Modern Language Association* , vol. 124, no. 2, March 2009 is a helpful overview.

30. For example, Richard C. Foltz, *Animals in Islamic Tradition and Muslim Cultures*, Oxford: Oneworld Publications, 2007.

31. Dale Peterson, *Eating Apes*, Berkeley and Los Angeles: University of California Press, 2003; Hiranmay Karlekar, *Savage Humans and Stray Dogs: A Study in Aggression*, New Delhi: Sage, 2008.

32. For example Henry Stephens Salt, *A Plea for Vegetarianism and Other Essays* 1886; repr., London Forgotten Books, 2018 that influenced Gandhi's ideas on the subject.

33. J.M. Coetzee, *The Lives of Animals*, Princeton: Princeton University Press, 1999; Timothy Findley, *Not Wanted on the Voyage*, Toronto: Harper Collins, 1984.

34. Graham Huggan and Helen Tiffin, *Postcolonial Ecocriticism: Literature, Animals, Environment*, London: Routledge, 2010. However, on the whole we do not give much importance to the ecocritics in our study because our primary concern is animals and their relationships with humans. Like gender and queer studies, ecocentricism had its philosophical roots in the activist movements of the 1960s and pairs its cultural analysis with moral commitment. It arose in tandem with modern environmentalism and then broke into

mainstream thought in the early 1990s as a reaction against the neo-Kantian idealism of the Yale School critics and New Historicists' politicization of nature and nature writing. For the New Historicists, nature is primarily a historical construct. The green theorists protested and insisted on the physical reality of nature as something that exists outside of and independent of human existence. Ecocritics, in criticizing the Yale School and New Historicists, tended to rebound into the opposite extreme, adopting a rigorously materialist position that assumes that it is our knowledge that alienates us from nature and that only a return to a pre-linguistic and pre-technological world will be able to arrest the industrial exploitation of our environment. They call to clean nature of 'conceptual pollution'. But, of course, unmediated contact with nature outside reason and language is an impossibility for humans. Reasoning beings cannot just 'switch off their rationality like a light bulb'. See Peter Heymans, *Animality in British Romanticism: The Aesthetics of Species*, New York and London: Routledge, 2012. Treating the entire non-human world as uniform is another problem with ecocritics. They do not make any ontological and moral distinctions between plant and animal organisms. In this way, they replicate the anthropocentric thinking they seek to explode. In any case, I think humans can try to study and understand animals beyond environmental concerns.

35. Marc R. Fellenz, *The Moral Menagerie: Philosophy and Animal Rights*, Chicago: University of Illinois Press, 2007.

36. Erica Fudge, *Animal*, London: Reaktion Books, 2002 greatly helped me to understand this. The following discussion is largely based on this book.

37. But on the other hand, Darwin's concept of sexual selection in terms of coy females and eager males

has been challenged. It is argued that there are no such fixed sex roles. Feminists have been particularly skeptical and vocal about this. Each male and female has her/his own temperament and behaviour.
38. Fudge, *Animal*, p. 127.
39. Donna J. Haraway, *Primate Visions: Gender, Race, and Nature in the World of Modern Science*, London and New York: Routledge, 1989.
40. Cited by Fudge, *Animal*, p. 130.
41. Ibid., p. 140.
42. In this connection one can mention 'deep history', a cutting-edge area of historical studies pioneered by Daniel Lord Smail. It re-bottoms human history to converge it with the history of life. Deep history treats our primate ancestors as significant historical characters, not on the basis of the same logic that has made the subalterns important in history over the past few decades, but to understand humans better by using analogies, identifying recurrent patterns and by making reconnections across time. See Smail's book *On Deep History and the Brain*, Berkeley: University of California Press, 2010 and Daniel Lord Smail and Andrew Shyrock, *Deep History: The Architecture of Past and Present*, Berkeley and London: University of California Press, 2011. Deep history seeks to understand human history in terms of brain and body chemistry. But it is not biological determinism, rather it challenges the biology-culture dichotomy. It talks about our biology-culture co-evolution and argues that human culture is embedded in the body, while at the same time the body is largely shaped by culture.
43. Vinciane Despret, 'From Secret Agents to Interagency', *History and Theory*, vol. 52, no. 4, 2013.
44. Bruno Latour, *Reassembling the Social: An Introduction to Actor-Network Theory*, Oxford: Oxford University Press, 2005.

45. Tim Ingold, *Perception of the Environment: Essays on Livelihood, Dwelling and Skill*, London: Routledge, 2011

46. Haraway, cited by Barbara B. Smuts, 'Between Species: Science and Subjectivity', *Configurations*, vol. 14, nos. 1–2, Baltimore, MD: The Johns Hopkins University Press, 2006.

47. Cary Wolfe, *What is Posthumanism?*, Minneapolis: University of Minnesota Press, 2010. The neurologist Damasio, *Strange Order of Things*, would support this.

48. David Gary Shaw, 'The Torturer's Horse: Agency and Animals in History', *History and Theory*, vol. 52, no. 4, 2013.

49. Ibid., p. 167.

50. Cited by Sandra Stewart, *Riding High: Horses, Humans and History in South Africa*, Johannesburg: Wits University Press, 2010.

51. Alfred W. Crosby, *The Columbian Exchange: Biological and Cultural Consequences of 1492*, Connecticut: Greenwood Publishing Group, 1972.

52. J.R. McNeill, *Mosquito Empires: Ecology and War in the Greater Caribbean, 1620–1914*, New York: Cambridge University Press, 2010.

53. William H. McNeill, *Plagues and Peoples*, New York: Anchor Books, 1976.

54. Human culture is, of course, important. But as we have seen, contrary to what Foucault says, all truth-claims are not culturally created and function as technologies of social discipline!

55. As Stephen Greenblatt has described the underpinning wish of historical research, quoted by Erica Fudge, 'Milking Other Men's Beasts', *History and Theory*, vol. 52, no. 4, 2013, p. 15.

56. Ibid., p. 16.

57. Ibid.

58. Shaw, 'The Torturer's Horse'.
59. Ibid., p. 164.
60. Chris Pearson, 'Dogs, History, and Agency', *History and Theory*, vol. 52, no. 4, 2013.
61. Thierry Hoquet, 'Animal Individuals: A Plea for a Nominalistic Turn in Animal Studies', *History and Theory*, vol. 52, no. 4, 2013, p. 89.
62. Laxman D. Satya, *Ecology, Colonialism and Cattle: Central India in the Nineteenth Century*, Oxford: Oxford University Press, 2004.
63. Gyan Pandey, 'Rallying around the Cow: Sectarian Strife in the Bhojpuri Region, c. 1888–1917', in *Subaltern Studies*, vol. 2, New Delhi: Oxford University Press, 1983.
64. John M. Mackenzie, *The Empire of Nature: Hunting, Conservation and British Imperialism*, Studies in Imperialism Series, Manchester: Manchester University Press, 1988; Mahesh Rangarajan, *India's Wildlife History: An Introduction*, Ranikhet: Permanent Black, 2001; Ranjan Chakrabarti, 'Tiger and the Raj: Ordering the Maneater of the Sunderbans, 1880–1947', in *Space and Power in History: Images, Ideologies, Myths, and Moralities*, Kolkata: Penman, 2001.
65. Samanta, 'Cruelty Contested'.
66. Mahesh Rangarajan, 'Animals with Rich Histories: The Case of the Lions of Gir Forest, Gujarat, India', *History and Theory*, vol. 52, no. 4, 2013.
67. These phases are called 'lion plague'. They occurred for various reasons in the 1960s and 1980s, not the least for policies of foresters. These phases saw lion attacks on livestock and sometimes even humans (Maldharis were targets in most cases) and poisoning of lions by irate humans, leading to a dip in the lion population.
68. David Quammen, *Monster of God: The Man Eating Predator in the Jungles of History and the Mind*, revd. edn., New York: W.W. Norton and Company, 2004.

69. Radhika Govindrajan, *Animal Intimacies: Beastly Love in the Himalayas*, New Delhi: Viking, 2019.

70. The people of Kumaon feel that they share the same experience of living in and being subject to the rules of Devbhumi, as Uttarakhand is often called. Similarly, while exploring the relatedness between humans and tigers in the Sundarbans, Annu Jalais argues that the fishermen there believe that they are tied in a web of relatedness with tigers, because they have the same symbolic mother in Bonbibi, and share the same forest products and the same harsh environment. See Annu Jalais, *Forest of Tigers: People, Politics and Environment in the Sundarbans*, Delhi: Routledge, 2009.

71. Radhika Govinrajan says, 'In India, the very notion of the native belonged to the grammar of animality and the colonial masters claimed that the animality and savagery of the colonized subjects made it necessary for them to protect nonhuman game; thus reserved the right to hunt to a select handful of colonists'. See Govindrajan, *Animal Intimacies*, p. 16.

72. Govindrajan cites Haraway's work on cyborgs and companion species to stress 'kin making is making persons' and that the process often goes beyond biology and genealogy. She further says that we can go beyond human realms to understand how life unfolds relationally.

73. Govindrajan, *Animal Intimacies*, p. 263.

74. A good summary of anthropological works in this area is provided by Molly H. Mullin, 'Mirrors and Windows: Sociocultural Studies of Human-animal Relationships', *Annual Review of Anthropology*, vol. 28, October 1999, pp. 201–24.

75. Anand Pandian, 'Pastoral Power in the Postcolony: On the Biopolitics of the Criminal Animal in South India', *Cultural Anthropology*, vol. 23, no. 1, 2008.

76. For example, Levi-Strauss's structuralist approach in understanding totemism.
77. R. Nelson, *Heart and Blood: Living with Deer in America*, New York: Knopf, 1997.
78. A number of writings have helped me understand this. I must especially mention the special issue of *History and Theory* cited earlier.
79. O. Oyewumi, *The Invention of Women: Making an African Sense of Western Gender Discourses*, Minneapolis: University of Minnesota Press, 1997, cited by Mallarika Sinha Roy in her essay titled 'Inside/out: Women's Movement and Women in Movements', in *Women Speak Nation: Gender, Culture and Politics*, Routledge, ed. Panchali Ray, Oxon and New York, 2020.
80. Pandian, 'Pastoral Power in the Postcolony', reveals this very well
81. Giorgio Agamben, *Homo Sacer: Sovereign Power and Bare Life*, Stanford: Stanford University Press, 1998.
82. Jacque Derrida, *The Animal Therefore I Am*, tr. David Wills, New York: Fordham University Press, 2008. This was originally a lecture that he delivered at a conference. The title of the lecture was 'The Autobiographical Animal'. Also see Sherryl Vint, 'Animal Studies in the Era of Biopower', *Science Fiction Studies*, vol. 37, no. 3, 2010, which draws upon Derrida's *The Beast and the Sovereign*, vol. 1, tr. Geoffrey Bennington, Chicago: University of Chicago Press, 2009.
83. Wolfe, *What is Posthumanism?* Also see his article 'Human, All too Human'.
84. Gautam Basu Thakur, '"A Strangeness beyond Reckoning": The Animal as Surplus in Postcolonial Literature', *Postcolonial Animalities*, ed. Suvadip Sinha and Amit R. Baishya, New York and London: Routldge, 2020.

85. Michael Lundblad said this in his edited volume *Animalities: Literary and Cultural Studies beyond the Human*, Edinburgh: Edinburgh University Press, 2018, cited in the Introduction to Sinha and Baishya, *Postcolonial Animalities*, p. 3. Sinha and Baishya's edited volume is an important contribution to postcolonial literary studies. It upholds Lundblad's approach and is about 'imaginaries of the human with grammars of animality', but claims to somewhat differ from Lundblad by showing concern for real animals, in both their 'materialist and representational renditions', their agency and alterity. The book largely conforms to postcolonial ecocriticism/zoocriticism by seeking to rewrite the biopolitical story of both humanity and animality.

86. Stefan Dolgert, 'Species of Disability: Response to Arneil', *Political Theory*, December 2010. Here he responds to Barbara Arneil, 'Disability, Self-image and Modern Political Theory', *Political Theory*, April 2009.

87. Martha Nussbaum, *Frontiers of Justice: Disability, Nationalisty, Species Membership*, Cambridge: Harvard University Press, 2007.

88. Gary L. Francione in *Animals as Persons: Essays on the Abolition of Animal Exploitation*, New York: Columbia University Press, 2008.

89. Barbara Arneil, 'Animals and Interdependence: Reply to Dolgert', *Political Theory*, vol. 38, no. 6, December 2010.

90. Arneil cites Daniel Engster for this.

91. Arneil cites Al Plumwood for this.

92. Arneil also considers the question of citizenship for animals and rejects the latter's claim in this regard too. She argues that we may consider Martha Nussbaum's suggestion that all severely cognitively disabled persons should be provided with 'proxy'

voters in elections to voice their interests, but animals cannot have proxy voters in the same way.

93. Kimberly W. Benston, 'Experimenting at the Threshold: Sacrifice, Anthropomorphism, and the Aims of "Critical Animal Studies"', *Publication of the Modern language Association*, vol. 124, no. 2, 2009.

94. In *History and Theory*, vol. 52, no. 4, 2013.

95. Fudge, 'Milking Other Men's Beasts'.

96. Govindrajan, *Animal Intimacies*, quotes Brian Massumi's *What Animals Teach Us about Politics*, Durham, NC: Duke University Press, 2014.

97. Govindrajan, *Animal Intimacies*, p. 261.

98. Herzog, 'Biology, Culture, and Origins of Pet-Keeping'.

99. Antonio Damasio says, 'Nothing short of a massive and enlightened negotiation between affect and reason could ever succeed'. See *The Strange Order of Things*, p. 220.

100. I have two questions for Govindrajan here: (1) Can there not be selfless love (famously called '*Krishnendriya preeti iccha*' in *Chaitanya Charitamrita* by Krishnadas Kaviraj, a biographer of Sri Chaitanya)?; and (2) Does it not occur to her that the women she portrays as loving animals and yet giving them away for ritual sacrifice or slaughter are under the grip of the overall culture (including its patriarchal aspect) they live in, to the extent that they have to justify violence in terms of this culture, going against their natural love, even to themselves? This is perhaps an example of how patriarchy, traditional social norms, cultural values, etc., seek to subjugate nature.

101. Schweitzer quoted by Ryan P. McLaughlin, 'Non-violence and Nonhumans: Foundations for Animal Welfare in the Thought of Mohandas Gandhi and Albert Schweitzer', *The Journal of Religious Ethics*,

vol. 40, no.4, 2012, 1965, p. 690. However, the word 'everything' in the first sentence suggests that he is considering not only animals but even inanimate objects in a kind of pantheistic approach to the world.

102. Agnes Heller, *The Theory of Need in Marx*, London: Allison and Busby, 1976.

103. This, of course, connects animal studies with postcolonial studies, reminding us of Gayatri Chakravarti Spivak's famous question 'Can the subaltern speak?' and her advocacy of a kind of politics that can give voice to those who cannot speak for themselves

104. Susan D. Jones, *Valuing Animals: Veterenians and Their Patients in Modern America*, Baltimore: The Johns Hopkins University Press, 2002.

105. Wendy Doniger, *The Hindus: An Alternative History*, New York: Viking Press, 2009; repr., New Delhi: Speaking Tiger, 2015.

106. Lance Nelson, 'Cows, Elephants, Dogs and Other Lesser Embodiments of Atman: Reflections on Hindu Attitudes Toward Nonhuman Animals', in *A Communion of Subjects: Animals in Religion, Science and Ethics*, ed. Paul Wadu and Kimberley Patton, New York: Columbia University Press, 2006.

107. Samanta, 'Cruelty Contested', p. 7.

Another kind of homologies connecting humans and animals in a timeless cosmic pattern in ancient India has been pointed out by Brian K. Smith. He shows how in Vedic society animal taxonomy posited an analogy between classes of beasts and classes in society. Different modes of animal taxonomy coalesced into a binary opposition between village/ sacrificial/edible, on the one hand, and jungle/non-sacrificial/inedible on the other. The human animal was the hierarchically superior of the *pashus*, and because of this superiority, he was considered unsacrificable and unconsumable. Some humans, particularly tribal people, were assimilated into the category of jungle animals, beyond the pale of humanity. Those humans who were assimilated into the category of village (domesticated) animals were subdivided into social classes, each linked to one or another of the non-human animals in this category. The quadripartite varna division of society was thus justified. A story depicts how Prajapati emitted from his head Agni among the gods, the brahmin among men, and the goat among animals; from his arms and his chest Indra among the gods, the kshatriya among men, and the horse among animals; from his belly the Visva Devas among the gods, the vaishya among men, and the cow among animals; from his feet not a single one among the gods, the shudra among men, and the sheep among animals. Brahmins were presented as the most voracious feeders on all other humans and not to be consumed by others (feeding means exploitation in this context). The kshatriyas could exploit the vaishyas who were actually equated with animals in general, particularly with the domestic animals they were charged with keeping. They were the natural food and prey for the two higher classes. The shudra, constituting the bottom rank, having emerged from Prajapati's feet, had to make a living by washing feet, i.e by serving others. Having no corresponding deity, he could not take part in sacrificial rituals. See Brian K. Smith, 'Classifying Animals and Humans in Ancient India', *Man*, vol. 26, no. 3, 1991.

108. Samanta, 'Cruelty Contested', Chapter 5. The present paragraph entirely derives from this chapter, particularly the section 'Animals, Vegetarianism and Humanitarianism'.

109. Bengali writers showed some concern from animals even beyond issues of vegetarianism and ahimsa.

Domestic animals in particular received their attention. Let me give some early examples. An article in the journal *Bandhav* talked about the virtues of dogs and cats, and how they served humans out of their own free will (unlike other animals who are forced to serve). However, it also pointed out the difference between the selfish freedom of cats and selfless freedom of dogs. See Anonymous, 'Kukkur o Beral athaba Swadhinata, Swarthaparata o Premer Katha', *Bandhav*, vol. 5, no. 2, 1287/1880.

Bhudev Mukhopahyay wrote an essay on the domestication of animals. At the outset he says how the survival of a non-human species depends on its utility for humans. Dogs, cats, goats, lambs, etc., are domesticated, because they serve humans. However, Mukhopadhyay argues, apart from their material benefit they can also enrich people spiritually. A keen observation of domestic animals would reveal that their feelings of joy and sorrow, aesthetics and ethics are largely similar to those of humans, and that 'intelligence' (*buddhi*) of humans and 'instinct' (*samskar*) of non-humans are actually the same. He argues that the Aryan authors of the Shastras were aware of this and they believed that all creatures were basically the same and took different forms according to their performance in their previous birth. He also mentions Western scholars' thoughts in support of this argument, thoughts that seems like pantheism from the way Mukhopadhyay describes it. Finally, he gives some advice regarding how to tame and take care of animals. See 'Pashwadi Palan', *Paribarik Prabandha*, 9th edn., Kolkata: n.p., 1326/1919. But the book was originally published in the nineteenth century.

Balendranath Tagore wrote an article on animals depicted in ancient Sanskrit literature. He shows how animals like swans, deer and cattle almost formed a part of human society and enjoyed human affection. He contrasts such portrayal of love, which was based on an easy acceptance of these animals, to the love for animals in the English poet Robert Burns' 'To a Mouse', where love seems somewhat exaggerated, because it is a conscious attempt at redemption amidst terrible cruelty to animals. Balendranath discusses Sita (in Bhavabhuti's *UttarRamacharita*) and Shakuntala's (in Kalidasa's famous play *Abhijnna Shakuntalam*) intimacy with animals in their ashramas. He also argues that though hunting was practised, it was restricted to the royalty and the poets' hearts bled for the animals killed. He cites the description of hunting in Banabhatta's *Kadambari* as an example. Finally, he exclaims, 'I am not aware if any other country in the world has such a religious ethic that goes beyond the humans and extends to the animal world.' He attributes this to a pantheistic worldview nurtured by the Hindus. See Balendranath Thakur, 'Pashupriti', in *Chitra o Kavya*, Kolkata: Adi Brahmo Samaj, 1301/1894. His uncle Rabindranath Tagore, however, did not quite like this piece, finding its claim somewhat contrived. See Rabindranath Tagore, in a letter included in *Chinnapatra*, cited by Pradyumna Bhattacharya in his essay 'Kalapahar: Natun Jatak?', *Sahitya Parishat Patrika*, vol. 14, 1999. Balendranath's claim for Hindu religion and its superiority was clearly motivated by the intense nationalist spirit of the late nineteenth century. Indeed, Bhudev Mukhopadyay's essay mentioned above shows a kind of nationalist pride too.

110. Jainism had an influence on Albert Schweitzer too, McLaughlin's article 'Non-violence and Nonhumans' is helpful for understanding both Schweitzer and Gandhi in this respect.

111. Sophie Kevany, 'Millions of US Farm Animals to be Culled by Suffocation, Drowning and Shooting', *The Guardian*, 19 May 2020, see https://www.theguardian.com/environment/2020/may/19/millions-of-us-farm-animals-to-be-culled-by-suffocation-drowning-and-shooting-coronavirus, accessed 15 February 2023.

2

Alternative Possibilities of Human–Animal Relationships in Bengali Literature

Introduction

From time immemorial animals have featured prominently in world literature and, even before that, in orature. Anecdotes about animals constitute a major part of folk tales, which were originally told when humans used to live in close proximity to animals. These stories are allegories of ourselves and our behaviour. They impute human speech as well as human qualities, both good and bad, to animals. They describe the human condition as well as relationships between humans and humans. They detail human situations of domination and subordination, conflict and compassion and usually have a moral to convey. *Aesop's Fables* are famous examples of this genre, as are *Panchatantra* and *Hitopodesh* of India. One would remember the story of the lion who tyrannizes all the creatures of the jungle until the clever fox makes him dive into a well and kill himself on seeing his own reflection there and mistaking it to be a rival lion.

A number of works of modern literature re-narrate such old folk tales for children. Here, *Tuntunir Boi* by Upendrakishore Raychaudhuri[1] readily comes to mind. Tuntuni, the little tailor-bird, made its nest by stitching together the leaves of a brinjal plant. There she had her three babies. However, a cat cast its covetous eyes on them. At first Tuntuni kept the cat away by flattering her. Later, however, as her babies learnt to fly, she no longer feared the cat and began to insult her. There are also many original stories in modern literature that anthropomorphize animals to make them more lively, to create a sense of fun, to entertain children and at the same time to generate in them certain values. We may even say that rather than anthropomorphizing animals, some of these stories zoomorphize human beings. In any case, many such stories are based on keen observation of animals and a sense of resemblance between humans and animals. Thus, they reduce the otherness of animals, reveal the sameness beneath difference and suggest a sort of kinship.

Indeed, stories from the ancient period detail humans living at peace among animals—from the story of Romulus and Remus raised as cubs by a pack of lions to Mowgli and Tarzan and more. In this chapter, however, we are not concerned with these categories of stories—stories of zoomorphized humans or anthropomorphized animals, which are full of fabulous events and create an atmosphere of magic realism. There are other kinds of animal stories as well—tales where animals are real and yet symbols of human bestiality. For examples, Kipling's 'The Undertakers' (1895) looks back on the great Rebellion of 1857. The heroic saga of an Englishwoman saving her child from the crocodile stands for the triumph of the British over their rebellious Indian subjects. The crocodile's defeat allegorizes India's colonial subjection.[2] There is also a genre of *shikar* (hunting) stories written in the Indian context in both English and vernacular languages, describing ferocious (though quite clever) animals and their killing by heroic hunters, thus catering to both British imperial and Indian aristocratic pride. We are not concerned with such stories either as they do not have any real concern for animals, serving only to illuminate human culture.

Another category of stories came into being from the nineteenth century. The origins of this category can perhaps be traced back to the English Romantic writers of the first half of the century.[3] This was a time when a commitment to animal welfare, even a sense of deep bonding with animals, was emerging thanks to the growing trend of pet-keeping and due to scientific insights into physical and emotional continuity between human and non-human animals. From the second half of the nineteenth century, English literature produced a variety of novels and stories about pet animals, mostly dogs and horses. R.M. Ballantyne's novel *The Dog Crusoe and His Master* (1861) and Anna Sewell's *Black Beauty* (1877) are early examples.

In Bengal, too, such modern sensibilities regarding animals emerged in the nineteenth century, and we have quite some stories of human–animal bonding from the 1920s/30s, of which we will analyse a few in this chapter. These are stories of real humans and real animals, though somewhat anthropomorphized. Although, some of the stories that we are going to discuss are perhaps open to double interpretations—animals as animals and animals as humans (e.g. Tarasankar Bandyopadhya's story 'Kalapahar')—all the stories chosen depict the reality of animal-human relationships and their nuances. They try to tell us how we humans, deep in hearts want to live with animals, a desire that usually gives way to melancholy. This is due to human culture coming into conflict with our inherent natural desire. Most of these stories have tragic endings with the animal dying, or rather, being sacrificed to maintain the human social order. We also notice paradoxes in the desire itself, based on the perception of our similarities and differences with animals—they are like us and yet quite unlike us. It is not only human culture that appears as a stumbling block in these stories, some point to the difference between humans and non-humans, which often defeats the efforts from both sides to reach out to the other. This particularly applies to stories of animals that belong to wilderness. However, most of these stories are about domesticated animals and their loving relationships with their owners, though tensions may be there even in such relationships.

The basic theme of all these stories is love, which makes life, both animal and human, worth living and wherein lies the beauty and sublimity of life. The stories take us to a world of universal kinship by portraying a soulmate-like relationship between animals and humans. Indeed, animals, in their pure and simple existence, are perhaps more soulful creatures than humans (though some humans have denied them precisely this). Thus stories of human bonding with animals take us to a soulful but lost world, or a world never really achieved, but can be glimpsed sometimes. Such human–animal love can easily transcend the species barrier as well as the barrier between nature and culture. However, there is duality or dilemma in this relationship too. Along with some loving humans, some indifferent and even cruel humans are present in the stories to create tensions. In these tales, it is generally the human species that jeopardizes the relationship. Often, the loving humans surrender to human culture, at least outwardly or temporarily, which results in tragedy. As the theme of the stories is love, they can become excessively sentimental at times. But to the extent they express the simple and pure truth of love, they can be appreciated. Indeed, some of them are considered classics in Bengali literature.

While the love between humans and animals may have always been present, its clear cultural expression can be traced only to the modern era. Animals like cats, dogs, birds, and cattle, have been a part of human life even in the premodern period, Still, our culture at its most sophisticated level, did not have much place for tender human–animal relationship for a long time, nor did they greatly feature in our literature (the Mangal Kavyas written in medieval Bengal, though, briefly deal with amicable relationships between humans and animals in passing, e.g. that between Lausen and his horse in the *Dharmamangal Kavya*). Thus, most early animal stories in modern Bengali literature spoke more about humans than animals while depicting this relationship. Yet, the way this relationship humanized humans bringing out the intensely compassionate elements of human heart took some of these stories to an amazing aesthetic height. Gradually, as days passed by, however, the animals' side of the story was presented more and more vividly by story writers, though of course, this was not a linear development that can be presented chronologically. A number of writers tried to construe situations according to the perspective of the concerned animal and thus rebuild the world as the animal perceived it. Occasionally, they attempted a complete reversal of the 'normal' direction of the dominant human gaze. A classic example is Bibhutibhushan Bandyopadhyay's 'Budhir Bari Phera', written in the mid-1930s, where the author seeks to present the perspective of a cow, who is the story's narrator. Compelled by human subjection to linguistic cognition, the authors chose to interpret the animals' gestures or the silent language of their eyes. Often, animal noises—a dog's bark or a cow's low— was roughly translated into human language. All this humanized the animals somewhat, which the authors evidently preferred to ignoring them altogether in the sphere of literature. Another common method of humanizing or anthropomorphizing animals is to give them a name. This makes the animal a person, practically giving it a status almost within the family. Most of the animal stories under discussion have the proper names of the animals as their titles.

The Bengali story writers approached the issue of human–animal relationships in more depth than animal studies scholars. The insights provided by animal studies can, of course, be found in the stories but there is more to them than that. We have seen in the first chapter how scholars of animal studies more or less agree that we are limited by our failure to know an animal's mind. The reason for this is that we believe in only language-based reason and reason-based intentionality. Thus, scholars urge us to shed our hubris and overcome our false sense of human exceptionalism to be able to know non-human animals better and empathize with them. For this, scholars recommend empathetic insights and sympathetic imagination. Fiction writers, with their sensitive minds and gift of imagination, are often better suited to this task. It may be argued that they practise (though only in their writing) what animal studies scholars preach. Recognizing the individuality of each animal and naming them is an important strategy suggested by animal studies scholars, and this is the very same strategy adopted by fiction writers as well. Recognizing an animal's individuality means recognizing its existential singularity; thus, the stories spontaneously make an animal appear as a subject and an agent—something that is not easy for animal studies scholars to achieve. After all, academics can never gain unmediated access into the inner workings of any agent's mind, human or otherwise, which litterateurs can image much farther to gain such insights. If the fiction writers have to somewhat anthropomorphize animals to achieve this goal, we have seen in the previous chapter how even that is encouraged by animal studies scholars for facilitating empathy and sympathy with animals. Sympathetic imagination is very important indeed for anyone to enter the mind of another being, because none of us can claim to know exactly how another feels, whether it is human or nonhuman; and yet there is an irresistible urge in us to try. Litterateurs arguably excel in the realm of sympathetic imagination. This brings to mind Rabindranath Tagore's short stories where he tried to empathize with women's feelings and greatly succeeded too. The gulf between humans and animals can be somewhat bridged in a similar manner. In *The Lives of Animals*, J.M. Coetzee says: 'There are people who have the capacity to imagine themselves as someone else, there are people who have no such capacity (when the lack is extreme, we call them psychopath), and there are people who have the capacity but choose not to exercise it.' While most people belong to the second and third categories, the fiction writers we deal with here belong to the first.

We have also discussed how animal studies scholars like Radhika Govindrajan ask us to 'move beyond anthropomorphism as regards ourselves: our inveterate vanity regarding our assumed species identity, based on the specious grounds of our sole proprietorship of language, thought and creativity'. Indeed, creative writers best know the limitations of language. The most powerful among them have sometimes found language inadequate to express their deepest thoughts. Tagore took to painting in the last decade of his life to depict moods of melancholy, harshness and conflict, which he thought were beyond the capability of his pen. One may also quote from Pam Houston's *Sight Hound* (2005) in this connection—words from a dog who is mocking humans:

Aren't the humans perfectly marvelous creatures? Doesn't it make you double over with laughter the way they remain committed to the idea that they're the only species that feels deeply, because—what—they have words to talk about their feelings? Has it not occurred to them that perhaps the reason they need so many words, the reason their words consistently fail them, is that they are so much poorer at interpreting their emotions than we are, that interpretation, per se, is a step that in the dog world we just skip?

The authors of these stories generally tried to rise above human cultural constraints to reveal the similarities between humans and animals and to express the latter's emotionality and intelligence. Just like humans, animals are portrayed forming habits, which are sometimes quite idiosyncratic.[4] Like humans, animals too get terribly upset when they are torn away from familiar surroundings and the people they love.[5] But above all, the writers stress the bodily existence of animals, their embodiedness, which, as animal studies scholars show, humans share with them and which ensures our continuity with animals. We find in these stories evidence of how bodily suffering and the need to respond to hunger or cold can bind humans and animals.[6] Sometimes a man's love for a woman becomes complicated by his love for a female snake or a cow,[7] thus portraying male-female love as something basic and 'beastly' and revealing the primeval animality of humans. In this way, rather than disavowing the animality of humans, some of the stories highlight it. Human–animal love in the stories largely rests on intercorporeality—staying close to each other's bodies, hugging, petting, stroking, licking, and so on. For the animal, of course, its bodily gestures are an important mode of communication. When animals resist and thereby assert their agency, they often do this through bodily resistance.[8] Their bodily dexterity, too, is highlighted in some of the stories. They are sometimes shown as very agile and athletic.[9] This is one aspect of intelligence that is clearly backed by physicality—a quality that is admired in humans, but called instinctual in the case of animals, as if innate instinct has nothing to do with the dexterity shown by Virat Kohli or Lionel Messi.

Above all, scholars of animal studies stress the political relevance of the body that forces us to confront our continuity with other animals. Biopower acts on both humans and animals, taking advantage of the bodily frailty and vulnerability of both. Indeed, animal studies scholars repeatedly tell us that domination and oppression of animals are often mediated by other hierarchies of difference, and that there are logical connections between speciesism, racism, sexism and other forms of oppression. To these we can add the specifically human forms of oppression like class difference, religious intolerance, etc. Thus, the sufferings of humans and animals due to human domination and oppression are depicted side by side in these stories. 'Mahesh' by Saratchandra Chattopadhyay is a famous example.[10] The story writers show, almost in the manner of Derrida, that more than a shared ability, it is rather shared helplessness and suffering that can bring a human and an animal together. Also like Derrida, they point out the singularity of each death, including that of an animal, and thus urge us to think about the animal with compassion.

A creature's bodily handicap often encourages the assertion of biopower by the powerful. In Bengali culture, Animals more often than not are hated and tortured even more if they are handicapped.

Therefore, physical disability is a common trope in some of the stories.[11] A story by Leela Majumdar, 'Manushder Galpo' (A Story of Humans), portrays disabled human characters and disabled non-human characters side by side in order to interrogate human attitudes towards both, almost in the manner of Stefan Dolgert, discussed in the previous chapter![12] And like Dolgert, it also puts forward an ethic of care premised on a theory of interdependency. The story ends with an animal hospital being set up in the locality and the caregivers there healing the two disabled children and their disabled pets mentally and also (partly) physically. The root of the ethics of care, the fact of emotional interdependency spanning both human and animal world, is also stressed in the story.

Indeed, most of the stories discussed in this chapter evoke the ethics of care and the underlying interdependency of humans and animals. Interdependency in the stories simply means that creatures need each other, because we all need to be needed. And animals sometimes fulfill this need of humans in a way that usually no humans can. Animals touch the primal core of our being, from where spring our basic emotions like love, fear, grief, hunger, bodily pain, etc. They can give us unconditional devotion and love, and can be our real soulmates. Of course, such interdependency is possible only between individual human beings and individual animals; it cannot apply generally to the species they belong to. However, a sort of inter-species dependency theory can perhaps be interpolated from this.

A common trope used by the writers to bridge the difference between humans and animals is to make a child the protagonist and set childhood against adulthood. Indeed, many of the stories were also meant for child readers. A child is yet to be fully socialized and belongs, rather, to the natural world. Indeed, childhood is one aspect of nature that modern humans tend to romanticize. Adulthood in this sense seems to bring with it a loss, a distance from the natural world. Thus, a part of growing up entails growing away from animals. Animals who come close to humans, on the other hand, are threshold creatures reflecting both culture and nature. Thus, in a number of stories, animals and children are paired in a relationship that seems to be superior to other human relationships. Children often adopt stray dogs or other animals against adults' wishes.[13] The child's openness in this respect is portrayed as superior to adult fear and skepticism. Eventually, the child protagonist triumphs and forces the adults to accept the animal, thus bringing the adults into fuller form of humanity. However, quite often, it is the animal who facilitates this by making the otherwise-unfeeling adults see its value through some sort of a crisis—protecting them from thieves or hooligans, for example.[14] But sometimes, the adults remain incorrigible and cruel, and the story ends in a tragedy.[15] In a number of stories by Tarapada Ray, animal characters (all sorts of animals - horse, donkey, cow, crow, snake) symbolize a lost and yet nostalgically remembered childhood.

In these stories, it is not only children who feel close to animals; adult women are also shown as more empathetic and sympathetic as are the poorer and comparatively uneducated sections of society, like the domestic help of upper and middle-class households and tribal people. This is perhaps because these people nurture a sense of indignity and humiliation in the face of the snobbery and injustice they encounter in society. One is also reminded of the thesis of Freud in this connection—children as well as tribal people feel closer to nature and hence to animals. Sigmund Freud, in his *Totem and Taboo*, argued that there is a great deal of resemblance between the attitudes of children and 'primitive humans' (read: tribal people) towards animals. Both children and tribals have no trace of arrogance that an adult civilized man has. They do not underplay their bodily needs and thus feel themselves more akin to animals. In a number of stories, poorer people develop intense emotive relationship with animals in contrast to the sophisticated upper/middle classes. In almost all the animal stories of Tarasankar Bandyopadhyay, the humans who love animals are very simple, poor and illiterate. In his story 'Suku o Bhuku', Bandyopadhyay directly points to the difference of attitude between tribals and the bhadralok (middle-class literati) towards dogs, particularly indigenous ones. The upper-class prejudice of favouring pedigree dogs and loathing mongrels is also criticized in quite a few stories; this is contrasted with the attitude of children and poorer people.[16]

Inverting the notion of superiority of culture over nature, the stories privilege the natural innocence of animals contrasting it with human evils, which is sometimes manifested in the form of zamindari oppression on poor peasants ('Mahesh' by Saratchandra), Hindu-Muslim riots ('Sada Ghora' by Ramesh Sen), and Partition which forced numerous people to become refugees (as in Tarapada Ray's stories). They show humans as flawed creatures, in contrast to whom animals are often projected as superior in terms of intelligence, emotional intensity, devotion, love, benevolence and valour. Animals are even shown converting ideas into purposeful actions and thus asserting themselves as agents. They often save the master/human friend or the latter's family members from danger.[17] Sometimes the animal even sacrifices itself to save its master.[18]

Occasionally, however, the animal's difference from the human world stands out and creates a tension in the relationship or puts an end to it. A domesticated animal is, after all a threshold creature, caught between nature and culture. The pull towards nature is more powerful for wild animals who come into close contact with humans and develop a bond with the latter. Thus, in Geeta Bandyopadhyay's 'Akash Patal', Bakuram, a Siberian duck, even after remaining in its host household as a family member for quite a few months, ultimately joins its fellow migratory birds on their return journey. In Bandyopadhyay's 'Bobby-r Bandhu', a baby bear captured from the forest is tamed with difficulty, becomes greatly attached to the little girl of the house, and yet remains unfathomable and unacceptable to most adults. Syed Mustafa Siraj's 'Jimmy', an otter, cannot but seem somewhat strange to the man who rescued and came to love him. Even dogs, the most domesticated of all animal species, sometimes creates problems, particularly if it is a mongrel. For example, Dibyendu Palit's 'Bhuli', a dog who cannot meet the standard of the middle-class household due to its habit of eating rubbish and therefore cannot be kept as a pet. However, it is perhaps such elements of difference that make these animals appear more fascinating.[19]

Some Early Stories: From Humanization of Humans to Humanization of Animals

Among the early stories, Rabindranath Tagore's 'Anadhikar Prabesh' (1894) cannot perhaps be called an animal story, though it prominently features an animal. 'Adarini' by Prabhat Kumar Mukhopadhyay, 'Mahesh' by Saratchandra Chattopadhyay and 'Budhir Bari Phera' by Bibhutibhushan Bandyopadhyay were written in the early decades of the twentieth century. These authors perhaps did not have much experience with the represented animals themselves, but through their sensitivity visualized an intense human–animal relationship. Bibhutibhushan went a step further and attempted to enter the animal's mind.

'Anadhikar-Prabesh' (Intrusion) is not about any enduring human–animal relationship. In the story, Jaykali is a widowed woman, a brahmin and owner of a temple. She was devoted to the god of the temple and was very keen on maintaining the precincts well. She was also known for her stern and strict personality. Though she was an expert in nursing patients, it is she who the patient dreaded most—she would not tolerate any laxity in their taking of medicine or diet. She had a nephew, who was like a son to the childless widow. But when the boy broke a creeper-shed in the temple garden, Jaykali ruthlessly punished him. One day, a dirty pig, chased by some drunken Doms (a Dalit caste) took shelter in the same creeper-shed out of fear for its life, thus rendering the temple impure. The temple priest tried to drive the animal away and the Doms started demanding their sacrificial animal. However, Jaykali shut the gates of the temple and shooed them away, shouting 'Don't desecrate my temple.' The Doms could not believe their eyes that an impure animal had found shelter in Jaykali's sacred temple of all places. Thus, 'this small incident pleased the Great God of all creatures, but the very small god of this small village, called "society" became highly aggrieved'. This is perhaps 'compassion' rather than 'love'. Nevertheless, the nature-culture dichotomy is brought out as this 'natural' form of compassion militates against the well-established religious norms of society.

'Adarini' (Dearly Loved), a classic short story by Prabhat Kumar Mukhopadhyay, written in 1913, focuses on a female elephant, but actually ends up saying very little about the creature. Jayram Moktar, an established lawyer with a thriving practice, buys the animal when his zamindar client hurts his pride by refusing to lend him his elephant for a wedding. Jayram's sense of prestige thus forces him to purchase an elephant from another zamindar. Over five years, the elephant, Adarini, becomes a sort of daughter to him. But as Jayram becomes old, his practice dwindles. As he requires money to get his granddaughter married, he is compelled to sell Adarini. It is his agony at parting with Adarini that is at the heart of the story. When well-wishers tell him to sell the elephant, at first he answers, 'Rather say, "You have to spend so much to feed your children and grandchildren—so sell them off!"' They argue, 'You claim that she is like your daughter. But you have to send off even your daughter to her in-laws' place.' When at last Jayram sends Adarini to Bamunhater Mela (a fair where animals are bought and sold), he feeds her sweets and says 'Adar, go and come back after visiting Bamunhater Mela' ('*Dekhe eso*'—usually in Bengal one bids farewell to a loved one not by saying *jao*, meaning 'go', but by saying *eso*, meaning 'come back'). Jayram cannot not bring himself to say goodbye. Indeed, Adarini returns after a couple of days, as no buyer has been able to afford her price. Jayram Moktar is rather pleased. People explain the return of the elephant through the mystical power of the word *eso* uttered by a good brahmin like Jayram. Very soon, however, Jayram is forced to send Adarini to another animal fair, which is bigger and far away. This time he does not even meet Adarini when the latter leaves the house. But Adarini becomes ill on her way to the fair and dies. When Jayram is informed of her illness and goes to see her, she is already dead. He falls over her carcass, cries inconsolably and says again and again, 'Your feelings were hurt, because I sent you off to be sold. That is why you have left me!' Jayram himself dies within a couple of months of Adarini's death.

In the story, there is only one description of the elephant's feelings—her reciprocation of this intense human love. When she is sent away for the second time, Jayram does not dare go near her. Instead, his granddaughter tells him that tears were running down Adarini's face when she left home. The old man sighs, lies down on the floor in grief and says, 'She knows. They can read others' minds. She knows she will never be able to return to this house.' On the whole however, the story tells us very little about the elephant's feelings, but it eminently humanizes the human protagonist.

Saratchandra Chattopadhyay's 'Mahesh' published in 1922 is about a bull who belongs to a poor Muslim sharecropper, Gafur. Mahesh and Gafur share the consequence of a terrible summer: drought, lack of food and drinking water and, above all, poverty. Their somatic needs, hunger above all, are unbearable for both of them. Their 'fleshy being in the world', their shared 'embodiedness', closely relate them to each other. They are thus deeply tied to nature. Culture on the other hand—with its brahminical hypocrisy personified by the brahmin zamindar and the brahmin priest Tarkaratna—accuses Gafur of starving his bull and holds him guilty for his religion (because Muslims usually consume beef). Gafur loves the bull deeply, who he has named Mahesh after Siva, a Hindu god. Even in adverse situations, he tries to feed Mahesh by removing straw from the thatched roof of his hut and even by giving the bull his own food and starving himself. But this is not enough to fill Mahesh's stomach. Tarkaratna threatens Gafur that if the bull dies of hunger, that is, if *gohatya* (cow-killing) occurs, the zamindar would 'bury him alive'. Indeed, as Gafur tries to sell Mahesh to the butchers (though ultimately he backs out), the zamindar calls him to his *sadar* (office) and rebukes him. Then, one day, Mahesh enters the zamindar's garden and, in a desperate state of hunger, wreaks havoc. The zamindar calls Gafur once again, this time beating him mercilessly. Gafur returns home and finds that Mahesh had pushed his daughter Amina, who was carrying a pitcher full of water. The animal was eagerly drinking water off the floor. In his anger, Gafur hits Mahesh's head with the sharp blade of his plough. Mahesh drops to the ground, is in terrible pain, and dies. Gafur then leaves the village with his daughter to work in a faraway jute mill.

While we do not learn much about the bull's perspective in this story, the account helps humanize the human. The short descriptions that we have of the bull are very physical: 'His deep black eyes are full of sorrow and hunger'; he destroys the neighbours' gardens to satisfy his terrible hunger; and finally the description of his death:

Mahesh tried only once to raise his head, then his starved thin body fell to the ground. A few drops of tears oozed out of the corner of his eyes, and a few drops of blood from his ears. His entire body trembled violently a couple of times, then he stretched his hind and front legs as far as possible and breathed his last. Amina cried out, 'What did you do, Baba! Our Mahesh has died!' Gafur did not move, nor replied. He stood like an immovably heavy stone and kept looking with his unwinking eyes at another pair of unwinking deep and black eyes.

The story contrasts the deep love between a Muslim man and his bull with the hypocrisy of Hindu brahminical culture that holds the cow sacred, but actually does not care a fig for the animal. It also draws a parallel between the cruelty of human culture towards humans and animals (in this case a bull).

In contrast to the above stories, 'Budhir Bari Phera' by Bibhutibhushan Bandyopadhyay written in the mid-1930s, tries to probe the mind of the animal protagonist. The work describes an old cow named Budhi, who no longer produces milk and hence is not considered worth keeping. Budhi is sold to some traders who take her to a slaughterhouse. Though she is unaware that she is in a slaughterhouse, Budhi feels very uncomfortable there and runs away. After a long and painful journey, she returns home to the delight of the little girl of the house, who is the only person there who loves her. Budhi was also welcomed by the girl's mother, who had not approved of the selling of the cow, perhaps (at least partly) for religious reasons: 'They sell cows to the slaughterhouses of Calcutta. You did not listen to me then—you thought this old cow does not give milk, so let's get rid of it by selling it. If this cow had died an unnatural death, would it have been good for this family?'

'Budhir Bari Phera' is a unique story in the sense that the author tries to enter the mind of the cow to describe her trauma, memories, relationships, happiness, etc. The story, thus, describes the way she resents the crowded and suffocating slaughterhouse, is scared by its terrible sounds and the smell of fresh blood, and repulsed by the cruel and greedy faces around her. She remembers her own house, the fresh sweet-smelling and delicious grass in the nearby pasture, and particularly the kind girl, Khuki. Next to Budhi in the slaughterhouse, there is a young cow, who is perhaps the age of Budhi's own eldest child. She feels affectionate towards him, but one day he is taken away, never to return. Budhi somehow associates this with the smell of blood and becomes even more scared. That evening she escapes. However, the journey home is traumatic. She is maltreated by people and even cows, which she resents most. As a big cow tries to butt her, 'Budhi felt deeply humiliated. She had never known that the world is so bad. Can't she expect a little sympathy even from her own species (*swajatiyas*)?—Insult by one's own species is unbearable. It is better to be killed by a tiger.' Of course, Budhi meets kind people as well who help her survive, but then they cannot do much for her because of the resentful attitude of their companions. One such person is a young housewife on a boat, on whose face Budhi can see compassion and humanism, who forces her reluctant husband and the boatmen to help the cow, as Budhi had fallen almost senseless into a marsh where she had come in search for water in her terrible thirst. The young woman also offers Budhi water to drink.

It is doubtful whether a cow feels particularly humiliated when maltreated by other cows, or whether she feels affectionate towards another cow because the latter reminds her of her long-begotten calf. These are evidently human-like thoughts. But in this deeply compassionate story, the author is successful in closing the gap between humans and animals. These days we often hear of old mothers being abandoned by their children and their consequent sufferings. Budhi's seems to be such a story. Bibhutibhushan used to campaign for the Hindu Mahasabha's cow protection movement. Perhaps the story was partly inspired by this political concern. However, it definitely reaches far beyond the realm of mere politics. The Hindu concern for cows is more often than not merely ritualistic (we have already seen this in the case of 'Mahesh'), and is used by some people for political capital. In contrast, in this story, the concern for cows is deeply compassionate.

Among other stories written during the 1930s are Tarasankar Bandyopadhyay's 'Kalapahar' and 'Nari o Nagini'. Kalapahar, the ox, is a fascinating creature (albeit a bit anthropomorphized), though perhaps the female snake in 'Nag o Nagini' is a means to explore both male and female psychology in a man-woman relationship. We will discuss both these stories in later sections. 'Kala' by Shailajananda Mukhopadhyay is another early story written in the mid-1930s. It is about a disabled dog that meets a tragic end. While the narrative describes Kala's loyalty and valiance, it does not tell us much about the dog's thoughts. Actually the story intends to reveal the inhumanity of the humans through this nonhuman character. We will discuss this story in a later section.

Differing Contexts and Varying Themes

The stories that are summarized in the following section spanned over a long period of time—from the late colonial period to the end of the twentieth century. But as their chronology does not seem that important, I have discussed them under some thematic headings (though perhaps even this thematic arrangement is somewhat arbitrary).

Peasant-Cow Relationships in Agrarian Culture

In the agrarian culture of the pre-tractor era, the relationship between a peasant and his cow was naturally very important, as highlighted in a number of Bengali stories[20] such as 'Mahesh' and 'Budhir Bari Phera', discussed earlier in this chapter.

Tarasankar Bandyoapdhyay wrote a number of short stories on this theme. Here is a classic one.Set in the 1930s, 'Kalapahar' describes the relationship between Ranglal, a Sadgop peasant, who is physically robust and hard-working, yet rough and obstinate to the point of being impractical in worldly matters, and his loving and beloved ox Kalapahar. Above all, the two are impractical in their love for each other. Pradyumna Bhattacharya, in an interesting article, observes that both Ranglal and Kalapahar stand for the roughness of the Rarh region, where Tarasankar came from, and where he set most of his novels and stories.[21] Ranglal adores Kalapahar, feeds him well, decks him up beautifully, and even massages his legs. Ranglal's son who has passed matriculation, does not like Kalapahar, nor does he appreciate the closeness between his father and the animal. After Kalapahar loses his friend—another ox named Kumbhakarna—he becomes violent in temperament, killing other bovines. Nobody except Ranglal dares go near him. At his son's insistence, Ranglal decides to take Kalapahar to a nearby cattle fair and sell him. This leads to tragedy.

Kalapahar does not speak any human languages, but he understands them. Above all, he understands the human mind and can communicate with humans even without speaking their language. For example, when he does not want to go where he is being led, he stands stolidly, fixed to the ground under his feet, and it becomes impossible for anyone to move him. This is how the ox expresses his objection. The author in his empathy can understand this language well and translates Kalapahar's bodily gestures as well as calls and screams into his own human language. When Ranglal leaves Kalapahar at the animal fair with the cruel *paikar* (trader), Tarasankar writes:

The paikar hit him once again. Kalapahar was madly looking for Ranglal everywhere. Where is he? No, he is nowhere. With a powerful pull Kalapahar snatched his rope from the paikar's hand and started running. This is the road. They have come by this road. He started running with his head raised high and desperately called aan-aan-aan! Kalapahar is running, and he is calling Ranglal: aan-aan-aan! But what is this? Where is he going? How far is his home?

This is a sort of dual voice, where the animal's and the author's voices become one.[22] It is the author's best attempt at resolving the paradox that animal consciousness and even the unconscious or subconscious can be revealed to us only through human language.

Ultimately the news of a mad ox running wild reaches the police sahib, who kills him. In his last moments, Kalapahar valiantly tries to fight with the police car, thinking it was another big animal like himself. Pradyumna Bhattacharya suggests that perhaps Kalapahar's confrontation with the English police official symbolizes the revolt of the indigenous people of the Rarh region. He particularly equates Kalapahar with the Santal rebels who challenged British rule. However, this is perhaps an overinterpretation. Bhattacharya is influenced by Tarasankar's later novel *Aranya Bahini* where the author mentions: 'They (the Santals) with red eyes like those of Marhatta oxen kept saying—give us back our girls.' Bhattacharya says that this perhaps gives a political dimension to Kalapahar's story. However, I think this unnecessarily delimits the significance of the story. Kalapahar is a deeply human story, that is all. But of course, the animal's tragedy here also reminds us of a common human tragedy. Love for another animal/human and for the places one is familiar with (topophilia) are important to the lives of both humans and animals. Today, we are all conscious about how eviction brings tragedy to human lives. Intimate forms of community fostered in the countryside come into acute conflict with large-scale projects of landscape engineering by the nation-state or big business. This disrupts the primordialist association between man and nature and violates their rights to the place. Similarly, the eviction of animals from familiar surroundings and from under the eyes of their beloved masters leads to tragedy not only in 'Kalapahar', but also in a few other stories discussed.

Tarasankar's 'Kamdhenu' is another story that revolves around a cow. Nathu, is not a peasant though, he is a Patua (a group of people in south Bengal who paint pictures and sing ballads based on them), has a *kamdhenu* (literally wishing cow, believed to be a daughter of Surabhi, the cow goddess; such cows are supposed to give milk without getting pregnant) and earns his livelihood by singing Surabhi Mangal (an epic in praise of Surabhi; the Patuas, though Muslim by religion, traditionally sing such songs) and by curing cow diseases in a rural area dominated by Sadgop peasants. However, Nathu is forced to sell the cow, named Surabhi, to a local family due to adversity caused by a terrible earthquake and a grievous famine, and also because he wants to marry Phulmoni, who demands a high bride price from him. However, he feels terribly unhappy and when after some time, he sees that Surabhi's health has evidently improved in her new home, strangely he feels even worse. He kills Surabhi by poisoning her. He then buys her hide from some cobblers and starts a new business of cow hide. He also sells off Phulmoni to another man. He fares well in his business. But one day, he kills a man who has killed a cow. This *goru-mara* (cow killer) had been doing penance by going door to door begging for alms while emulating the low of the cow. Hearing this, Nathu gets angry and kills him. This is perhaps a sort of self-punishment for him. As a result, Nathu is given a death sentence. Even in his prison cell his obsession with Surabhi remains strong and is expressed in abnormal behaviour. In the story, Phulmoni and Surabhi are placed side by side in the context of Nathu's love life. His love for both, woman and cow, borders on perversion. This is, however, a story in which the human protagonist and his psyche are more important than the animal. Though we learn that Surabhi is an exceptional cow, we do not get any insight into her mind.

'Harbola's Daak' by Abul Bashar is a comparatively recent story and is set against a comparatively recent agrarian background. The title refers to the sounds of a *harbola*, meaning one who can mimic various voices and sounds. The story takes its cue from Saratchandra's story 'Mahesh' and also uses a dramatized version of it for its central theme. Like 'Mahesh', it highlights the sufferings of a poor peasant's life, which is shared by the peasant's cow. Only the background to this story is more recent. However, it is not a very modern background and it depicts rural life at a time when tractors were yet to be introduced, and hence peasants had to depend solely on cows and ploughs to till their land. Here the peasant is seen to spend the whole day by talking to his cow, and the story writer remarks: 'In the whole field, what other living existence did the peasant have? He is a primeval existence himself, and his cow is a similarly primeval creature, thoroughly loyal.' In the story, a schoolteacher, Moulik, decides to have 'Mahesh' staged by his students. The role of Mahesh, the ox, is to be played by Siben, alias Bharul. He is not to be seen on stage but as a *harbola*, he must remain hidden and emulate Mahesh's low according to the latter's various moods—when his master Gafur fondles him, when he is hungry, and finally and most importantly, when he is about to die. Moulik says, 'Unless you understand the relationship between a man and his cow, you cannot understand the story "Mahesh". This is most important. Bharul is the son of a peasant. If he can understand deeply his father's relationship with their two oxen, only then he will be able to take this drama to a climax, and life and drama will become one.'

Bharul listens to his teacher attentively and remembers that one of their own oxen also has deep black eyes full of melancholy and hunger. Bharul's father is a poor peasant with only 3 bighas of land. Moreover, two consecutive years of flood has damaged his harvest. Till very recently he could not feed his oxen properly and superstitiously believed that Kelo, his black ox, was responsible for his ill luck. This particular black ox had been purchased with the help of a bank loan. Bharul's father was very worried about repaying the loan as it carried a high interest rate. The bank had sent its jeep twice to remind him about his payments. However, as luck would have it, a year later, Bharul's father was able to reap a good harvest. This had now made the black ox his favourite. Bharul has no problem in identifying Mahesh with Kelo. He closely observes Kelo's behaviour and sounds to prepare himself for the role of Mahesh.

Unfortunately, however, Kelo becomes seriously ill. Bharul knows that the basic cause of his illness is poverty, and that his death will be poverty-related, just like that of Mahesh. He helplessly observes Kelo's sad death. The ox tumbles to the ground with a violent force, his tongue hangs out, his legs tremble and he gradually become still. He lets out a strange cry—'*Ma go*' (in human language it sounds like someone calling for their mother in distress), hearing which Bharul's mother comes running. But the ox cannot be saved. While Mahesh died silently, Kelo calls out *Ma go* at the time of death. With a heavy heart, Bharul notices the difference. He remembers Moulik Sir's words: 'You are not being able to reproduce the sound of a cow at the time of death. You have never seen a poor peasant's cow fall to the ground and die. You are excellent in copying all other sounds, but not the sad and terrible sound of death. One needs experiences in life to do certain things. Drama is not a fancy thing.' Bharul's heart breaks while remembering these words.

The next day, Bharul and his father take the carcass of the ox to the bank on a bullock cart to show the bank officers that it had actually died. That very night he excels in his performance of Mahesh at the school theatre. At the same time as Mahesh's on-stage death is being performed, a rich peasant family brings home a new red tractor. The sound of the tractor threatens to make Mahesh's low almost inaudible. However, raising his voice above the sound of the tractor, Bharul cries out again and again '*Ma go!*' Here, the tractor symbolizes the end of an age when farming was based on an intimate relationship between the peasant and his ox.

The Triumph of Mongrels over Pedigreed Dogs

Most dogs in Bengali literature are strays and of indigenous breed. Stray dogs triumph over expensive foreign breeds in these stories, going against our culture which privileges the latter over the former. This subversive process is usually initiated by children in the stories, who are yet to be fully incorporated into the culture they are born into, are closer to nature and thus feel strong connections with dogs. Sometimes even the adults come to accept the stray dogs eventually. This happens after the dog helps humans overcome some sort of crisis through its loyalty, intelligence and valour.[23] Let us look at some of these stories now.

'Doggie: Alsatian Noy' (Doggie: Not an Alsatian) by Tarasankar Bandyopadhyay interrogates the culture of undermining indigenous dogs. Ratan, a college student, buys a pup from a man who tells him that it is an Alsatian. Ratan gives the pup a fashionable foreign name—Doggie. But Doggie turns out to be an ordinary indigenous dog (called *neri* in Bengal). He makes friends with two street dogs and loves playing with them in a typical *neri*-like manner: 'Two of them fight by way of playing. One of them stands aside and watches, and seems to be smiling—"Fine!" He watches like a serious referee to take note of fouls.' Ratan tries his best to train his dog and make it no less than an Alsatian. To achieve this, he beats the dog ruthlessly.

As a result, as soon as he sees Ratan, the dog would lie down on its back and raising his legs high start barking, the meaning of which is either 'Oh don't beat me, I plead you' or 'I will never do it again, I promise you!' Its tail that is always up with a 'Don't care' attitude even to the sun and the moon, would immediately coil between its legs on seeing Ratan, and with his head moving funnily with a 'kuin kuin' sound the dog would beseech Ratan—'Oh master, I'm not an Alsatian. I don't have that much of intelligence. If you beat me, I would rather die; but it is not possible for me to become an Alsatian'.

One day, a thief enters the house. Doggie does not bark, but bites his ankle and thus helps the family catch him. The thief turns out to be the man who sold the dog to Ratan. When the man exclaims—'Oh, how devilish this dog is! It did not bark at all!'—Ratan says, 'That is because it is not an Alsatian, but an indigenous dog. This is his way of catching thieves.' When Ratan fondles Doggie for catching the thief, the latter's friends relish the sight. 'Probably they were smiling, at least it seemed so.' At last, Doggie and his friends are admired and appreciated not only by Ratan, but by his entire family.

'Suku and Bhuku' is another such story by Tarasankar. A pup from the street, perhaps abandoned by its mother, takes shelter in the house of Suku, a little boy. The pup first draws the attention of the household servants, and though they are initially reluctant to keep it as a pet, they ultimately take pity on it. When Suku first sees the pup, he is highly amused by the way it lies down on the floor and responds to Suku's fondling by moving its head from side to side, by the way it opens its mouth to show its teeth as if smiling, and by the way it thumps the floor with its tail. The pup is named Bhuku. As it grows up, its *neri*-like behaviour—eating rubbish, and returning home smeared in filth—irritates Suku. One day he beats Bhuku mercilessly and the pup runs away, never to return. Suku and the maidservant of their house feel bad about this as they both love the pup.

After a couple of years, however, Bhuku returns to the locality as a beautiful healthy dog, accompanied by a Santal youth. Suku recognizes him and the dog too jumps and dances in glee on seeing his former master. But when Suku claims 'It is my dog', the Santal castigates him and says:

No, he is not your dog, he is mine. I know he was yours. But you turned him out having beaten him. He was a little pup then. I happened to be visiting a relative's house in this locality. I picked him up. I took him in my arms and carried him three miles to my home. You broke his leg. I gave him medicine and cured him. I realized that he was of a good breed. Now you see a fine dog and claim it to be yours. Come Tungri, come. Let's go.

The difference between tribal culture and the mainstream bhadralok culture with regard to their attitude towards dogs (particularly indigenous ones) is revealed in this story. It is also clearly shown that the person who loves Bhuku most in the middle-class household is not a family member nor is it Suku, on whose insistence the dog was kept as a pet; in fact, it is the maid servant. The poorer and less sophisticated people's capacity to love animals more is once again revealed here.

'Pintu' by Saradindu Bandyopadhyay is about a thin and timid mongrel, often seen with his tail between his hind legs when chased by the dogs of another locality. However, he is a good 'retriever', and hence an invaluable companion to his master on the latter's hunting trips. The story describes how Pintu valiantly saves his master from some evil supernatural force at the cost of his own life. Apart from loyalty, Pintu's power of communicating with his master is also stressed in the story. He tries his best to prevent his master from further encountering the danger lurking in the jungle—again and again he would run towards the village and come back to his master, appealing to the latter with his eyes. 'Dogs cannot speak, but Pintu seemed to be telling me clearly—"Let's go back. This is a very bad place".'

Dibyendu Palit's 'Bhuli' focuses on a stray dog of the same name. In Bengali stories, stray dogs are often named Bhuli or Bhola, referring to something to be forgotten, of negligible importance. Still, this name individualizes a dog. Even Bhuli was aware of this: 'A dog as she might be, she knows the advantage of having a name, and of course takes this advantage to the full.' The small boy who narrates the story calls out 'Bhuli' to offer her leftover food from their house. Though other street dogs come running along with her, Bhuli drives them away: 'Babu has called me, not you.' Of course, this is the boy's interpretation of Bhuli's behaviour. However, this sort of animal-animal and even human–animal communication is quite possible:

Though there is no similarity between human and dog languages, yet Bhuli could easily understand what I wanted to tell her, and I could easily understand what Bhuli wanted to tell me. Funnily, I learnt something of the dog language from Bhuli. For example, 'bhuk' means 'flies', 'kuin kuin' means 'oh, I'm sorry', 'bhou-rrr' means 'take care'.

One night, when the boy's father returns home late, Bhuli saves him from hooligans in a deserted street. But Bhuli is dirty, used to eating rubbish, so she cannot be kept as a pet, despite the boy's eagerness. Then, one day, Bhuli becomes a mother. The way she looks after her three pups and calls for help to save them on a rainy night, makes her look almost human in terms of intelligence and motherly compassion. But tragedy strikes. The boy's uncle beats Bhuli and she runs away. Two of the pups are killed by a fox in their mother's absence. But the one that remains is taken in as a pet. The story thus ends in a cultural compromise: Bhuli is already grown up and, hence, has developed bad habits; but the pup can perhaps be trained properly.

Confusion and contradictions in human–animal relationship are thus revealed. The liminality of stray dogs, in particular their intermediate position between civilized association and degraded state often becomes disturbing for humans. On the one hand, by showing some admirable and superior qualities, they often challenge the hegemonic values of human society. On the other hand, unless they modify their behaviour by complying with human standards, they cannot be fully accepted by humans. But of course, the small boy of the house feels for the animal more intensely than his guardians. When the uncle beats Bhuli, the boy deeply sympathizes with her. Bhuli's qualities, including motherly love, are highly appreciated. She is particularly admired for her athletic qualities—from the way she tackles the monkeys who descend to the boundary wall of their house from the tamarind tree, it seems 'if she had been a human being, she would have got a chance to play for a reputable soccer team'. If athletic qualities are admired in human beings, they surely must be admired in animals as well.

'Bhow Bhow Yap Yap' by Leela Majumdar is another story pitting street dogs against pedigreed ones and favouring the former. In this tale, a street dog dies, leaving behind two pups. Two orphans, who live with their grandparents, take pity and bring them home. At first, no one in the house likes the pups. The maid Bamunmasi wants to turn them out, but the children persuade her to keep them, saying, 'Oh, their mother has died. How can we throw them away? Our mother has died too. Will you then throw us away?' In this case, orphanhood is perceived as a source of empathy. The grandmother does not like the pups either but allows them in. The grandfather is of an aristocratic temperament and is absolutely opposed to keeping stray dogs. He prefers pedigreed dogs only. Thus, the children have to hide the pups from him. But the ambivalence of bhadralok culture (including nationalism) is sharply questioned in this connection. The children thus reflect on this culture: 'Foreign dogs are good and indigenous dogs bad—what sort of argument is this? We are indigenous too. Dadu himself admires the scarlet-bordered dhoti and decoratively creased Punjabi, because they are swadeshi.' One day, a man comes to Dadu and sells him a dog named Lord claiming that that it is of a high pedigree. He says that his sahib's bitch had five pups, and the sahib told him to kill three by drowning them in water. But he did not have the heart to obey the sahib and decided to sell them. However, the man is actually a thief. At night, he breaks into their house to steal valuables. The street dogs Udo and Budho bark fiercely and help the children catch the thief.

'Kukul aar Elomelo' by Geeta Bandyopadhyay is, for a change, a light and enjoyable story. It describes the delightful adventures of two pups. The first is an orphan street dog, brought home by the compassionate author and named Kukul. The man who brings the second pup to the author says mysteriously but actually perhaps insightfully, 'If you want to keep a dog as a pet, you have to become a dog yourself.' This second pup is named Elomelo. 'Elomelo, is very civilized. He knows what all he should not do. And hence before he does any such wrong thing, he wags his hairy tail (in his language, it is like saying "Sorry, Sir!") and then embarks upon the battlefield heroically.' The story describes the destructive ventures and antics of Kukul and Elomelo. The author is apparently perturbed, but actually highly amused.

Revealing the Primeval Animality of Humans and Animals

'Jantab' by Narayan Gangopadhyay is another story about the relationship between a man and his dog. However, this tale focuses on the man and we do not know much about the animal in the relationship. The story is unique in the sense that rather than humanizing the dog, the story brings out the animality of its master. It reveals how humans and animals share the same bodily—or rather, beastly—needs (*jantab* means beastly). It describes how the common feelings of hunger, cold, etc., make humans and animals very similar. It also shows the contradictions within human–animal relationships. Even a dog, known to be man's best friend, can become his competitor if the situation demands it. If man-woman love is primeval and beastly, so are human–animal relationships.

In 'Jantab', a tribal who is ditched by his wife kills her lover and leaves human society to live a solitary life in a cave in the Himalayas. The local people call him Gumpha Lama, give him alms, and believe that he is not really a man but a supernatural entity. He has been living this way for thirty years. The treachery of his wife and perhaps his loneliness make him violently inclined. In his old age his only companion is a dog named Lallu, certainly more faithful than his wife. The story unfolds against the background of a terrible storm, with rain raging for days without respite. Both the man and the dog begin to starve. The fire in their cave goes out, and they try to survive by staying close to each other and thus keeping themselves warm. But the man resents the dog trying to get under his only blanket, which is torn and not big enough to accommodate them both. He kicks the dog ruthlessly. But the dog is desperate as well. He now seems to be in a violent mood. Lama hits him with a stone and then pushes the dying dog down the hill. The next day, the weather clears and Lama regrets killing his only friend in the world. He goes down the hill in search of Lallu. However, in a strike of fate, he is killed by a pack of wild dogs.

Tarsankar's 'Nari o Nagini' portrays the love between an ugly, lame snake charmer named Khonra Sheikh and a female snake— which Khonra's wife Zobeda does not like at all. Khonra loves his wife deeply, but he also, in a way, falls in love with the snake. Khonra calls the snake Bibi, pierces her snout to make it wear a nose ring, hangs her around his neck, kisses her and says, 'Even they love, Zobeda. I have extracted her poison-fang, but after all she has teeth, yet never does she bite me.' He even puts vermilion on the snake's head and tells Zobeda, perhaps jokingly, 'I have married her, she is you co-wife.'

Such animal stories occasionally bring out the animal's closeness to nature, something which humans have sadly lost. Khonra's snake is an Udaynag, a category of snake that greets the rising sun by expanding its hood towards it and playing merrily. The day Khonra caught the snake, 'it was so engrossed in playing and felicitating the sun, that it did not hear Khonra's footfalls'. This is how Khonra was able to catch the snake. During the mating season, however, Khonra has to free the snake, though he feels sad about this. But at night the snake returns to their room. Zobeda then hits her with a cow-dung cake and she flees. Later at night, the snake returns to bite Zobeda, who dies in the morning. Khonra considers this Bibi's revenge. He is about to kill the snake but does not have the heart to do so. He sets her free saying, 'She is not really guilty. This is the nature of females. Zobeda did not like you too.' Even if the story establishes the snake's attachment to Khonra, it remains doubtful whether biting Zobeda was a consciously revengeful act on its part.

In most cases, human–animal love seems closer to paternal or maternal affection from the human's perspective. Sometimes, however, it is portrayed as parallel to male-female attraction, another basic instinct common to most species. Tarasankar wrote quite a few such stories elaborating on this aspect of human–animal relationships. 'Kamdhenu', which we have already touched upon, is about a human whose love for a cow seems to be a sort of psychopathy, but perhaps belongs to this category.

Questioning the Human View of Animals and the Disabled

Both animals and disabled humans are looked down upon by able-bodied human beings in terms of deficiency and abnormality. If the animal is disabled as well, human loathing towards it is doubled. On the other hand, physical disability may enable some humans to empathize with animals. In the story 'Nari o Nagini', discussed above, the male protagonist is lame, which is at least partly responsible for his closeness with the snake. In the first chapter of this volume, I mentioned that American animal scientist Temple Gardin claimed that she could comprehend a cow's view of the world better because of her own autism and, based on this insight, tried to redesign abattoirs in America to improve the experience of cows that were going to be killed. Anna Sewell, author of the famous novel *Black Beauty*, became crippled at an early age due to an accident. For greater mobility, she was forced to use horse-drawn carriages. Her own helplessness made her sensitive to horses as fellow creatures. I will now summarize two stories from Bengali literature on disabled animals.

'Kala' by Shailajananda Mukhopadhyay is a telling story about human cruelty towards a disabled animal. What makes it seem all the more cruel is that in this story the disability of the dog is caused by human negligence. Johny, the pet dog, is for a change a beautiful pedigreed one, but its pedigree soon gets offset by its deafness. This is not congenital deafness. During a marriage ceremony in the house, the dog was kept in the attic for a few days without proper food and water, which led to its deafness. From then onwards, the humans of the house resented the dog. Even Anil, the boy who was Johny's master, became ashamed of it. Johny was renamed Kala (meaning deaf). They even turned it out of the house, after which it started living on scraps of food thrown away by people. But it did not stop acting as the family's watchdog and one day even saved them from burglars, who wounded it with a spear. Even this failed to arouse the pity of the family members, except perhaps Anil. Gradually, the dog became irritable in nature and started biting people, which increased human resentment towards it. The other dogs in the locality used to attack the helpless dog as well. Ultimately, the boy's uncle shot Kala and thus got rid of the dog. Anil saw other boys of the locality laughing and merrily pulling Kala with a rope. 'Kala's half-closed eyes were looking at him pitifully. The wound on its belly made by the spear of the burglars, which was yet to dry, has been freshly hit by the bullet and made the dog's chest red with blood.'

In contrast to most of the stories discussed here, 'Manushder Galpo' by Leela Majumdar has a happy ending. It is the story of a little lame girl named Lachhmi who is teased by everyone in school as well as at home, except her grandfather and her lame dog Bhulo. Their love is the only consolation in Lachhmi's sad life. One day, while taking Bhulo for a walk, she meets a small boy Felna whose left hand is defective and who keeps a blind cat, Mao, and a lame duck, Pnak Pnak as his pets. Lachhmi and Felna empathize with each other. Felna introduces his pets to Lachhmi. The cat Mao, a great fighter, never gave up on a fight even though he had lost one eye and an ear. And then there was the duck Pnak Pnak, who had been caught by Amu Chacha to roast it for his dinner. But the duck had pecked at Amu Chacha's head and made him bleed. Amu Chacha broke its leg in retaliation. Then it was adopted by Felna.

Though, both Lachhmi and Felna believe most humans are bad, eventually they change their opinions, as a veterinary hospital is built in the neighbourhood. The human nurses and doctors become friends with them and cure the defective limbs of their pets, except for Mao whose blind eye and torn ear remain, and so does his quarrelsome nature. In this story, human cruelty not only towards animals, but also to physically handicapped humans, is interrogated with a vision to have a better relationship.

If living is basically 'physical', humans and animals share that experience of physicality and hence also any physical handicap they may have. This explains Lachhmi's empathy with Bhulo, and the feelings both Lachmi and Felna have for their respective handicapped pets. Both of them believe that the actual handicap is, more often than not, augmented by human cruelty.

Animals are ordinarily regarded as disabled (deficient, inferior, less than human); if they are physically disabled they are subjected to all the more cruelty, as the story shows. The tale questions the way human society views disability (see the arguments of Dolgert in the first chapter). An anomaly in human nature is brought out in this connection. Humans are proud of their intelligence and look down upon animals for not having it; yet, they are cruel to the physically disabled. Instead of helping them make up for that disability by application of their mental capacity, they tease and torture the disabled.[24]

Human Evils in Contrast to Animal Innocence

In a number of stories, the evils of human society stand out in clear contrast to the innocence of animals. In fact, no creatures can be as cruel as humans. Some of the stories we have already discussed can once again be cited in this connection, for example 'Mahesh' or 'Kala'. Here are two more such tales.

'Sada Ghora' by Rameshchandra Sen is about a white horse that takes refuge in an unknown locality during the pre-Partition communal riots, having lost his shelter and master. He becomes popular among the youths of that locality. They pat him and ride him, but nobody cares much about feeding him. He pines away and becomes ill. Then, one day, a poor old man wearing a lungi and a fez appears. He recognizes the horse as his own and the horse instantly recognizes him as well. The man is the horse's syce and coachman. He feeds the horse and it immediately seems to feel better. He asks a local gentleman, 'When will peace be restored, Babu? Then I can start running my cart again.' But suddenly a rumour spreads that a riot had broken out in a neighbouring locality. Armed and violent people come running in search of Muslims to kill. The old syce is scared. Even Sohrab, his horse, can feel the impending danger and become melancholic. The syce is taken inside a house by local people and given protection; however, the horse remains outside. After an hour, the army arrives and the riot stops. People come out of their houses and find Sohrab dead.

The horse is lying on the road. His white colour seems all the more dazzling against the black tar of the road. His body is on the road and head on the pavement. There is a round wound by the side of his right ear. Sohrab is looking at the sky. His look is as pure as the diamond-like transparent sky.

The white horse here is a metaphor of love and innocence, signifying the beauty and nobleness of life, against which human violence seems irrational and immoral. An animal, thus, reveals both the meanness and the greatness of humanity during times of war. But at the same time the animal is a real creature and not just a metaphor. The bond between the old man and his horse seems absolutely natural.

'Idu Mianr Morga' by Narayan Gangopadhyay is a delightfully comic story, in contrast to most animal stories in Bengali literature. Idu, a butcher, refuses to kill a particular castrated cock, for it once sought protection from him while being chased by some of his family members who intended to cook it.

Perhaps the cock somehow felt—in the way all creatures feel—the reason why a cow refuses to move when the butcher comes and pulls the rope around its neck, or a goat cries out even before the knife is brought out—perhaps for the same reason the cock tried to run away. But when it realized that there was no chance of escape, it came running to Idu Mian and took shelter in his lap. Idu was about to strangle it. But suddenly he stopped. The cock was trembling out of a strange fear, it was looking at him with a helpless appeal in its eyes, it was trying to find comfort on his chest like a scared child.

Idu kept the cock as his pet, much to the chagrin of his wife and others who wanted to kill it for food. When people cast their covetous eyes on the cock, Idu thought disgustfully, 'Is there nothing in this human world (*samsar*) but a lot of greedy tongues?'

The story then takes a comical turn. One day, a *dafadar* of the local police station, a powerful man, forces Idu to part with the cock, which of course moves him to tears. The *dafadar*, in turn, is forced to hand it to the Officer-in-charge (OC) of the thana. Then, an inspector comes to visit the thana and takes the cock away. Ultimately, however, the cock manages to escape and the inspector fractures his leg in his attempt to catch it. The cock returns to Idu Mian, to the latter's delight.

The conclusion of the story is as follows: within a few days, the OC is suspended for taking bribes, the *dafadar* is sacked for dereliction of duty, and it takes three months for the inspector's fractured leg to heal. The story presents the message that humans are no better than a mere cock; the only difference is that they can assert their power over each other and over animals more effectively. If humans have one commendable quality, that is love.

'Putreshti' by Jyotirmoyee Devi is an indictment of the desire for male children that sometimes leads to extreme irrationality and terrible cruelty in Indian society. The story features an innocent animal to reveal this. A wealthy elderly couple has two married daughters, but no son. They are desperate for a son, who will be their heir and inherit their property. They arrange for a *putreshti yajna*, a ritual sacrifice performed in front of fire to pray to the gods to gain a son. The animal in the story is a baby bear named Tipu, a household pet who has been brought from Burma by the man along with some other animals. This is mentioned early in the story, but we do not hear about the bear again until the time of the yajna. The sadhu who performs the yajna insists on having the bear as the sacrificial animal, as, according to him, the sacrificial animal should look somewhat like a human because the future son would largely resemble it. The man, who loves the bear dearly and plays with it regularly, reluctantly agrees, yielding to the desire of his wife (who is afraid that her husband would remarry if she did not give him a son). The bear is brought to the sacrificial site, where a pit has been dug for him to be buried alive. The baby bear appears in the story briefly, but in a telling manner. He is scared and does not want to descend into the pit. He is lured into the pit with a banana and, holding the assuring hand of his owner, descends. He is given more fruits while the ritual goes on. After receiving a signal from the priest, ten people start filling the pit with baskets of earth. The bear makes a desperate attempt to escape, but in vain. The spot that covers the pit continues to shake for some time even after it is completely filled and the sacrificial fire is lit on it. The bear's master sheds a few tears, which are attributed to the fire by those present. The man falls ill after the ritual and does not live for long. A son is born to the couple and is thus described: 'The head is rather long, the hands are longish too, with lots of hair on hands and legs. He has a blank idiotic look. His speech is slurred'. Therefore, the couple's daughters have to return to their parental home with their husbands to look after the property. A rumour is rife that the man often dreamt of the baby bear before the birth of the son, which once again reflects the superstitious culture of orthodox society. A sensitive reader would, however, like to think that the conclusion of the story was imagined by the author as a retribution for the killing of an innocent and trustful creature, through deception, and thus letting cruelty triumph over love in order to yield to the unreasonable pressure of a patriarchal culture.

Finding One's Lost Childhood and Lost Land in Animals

Stories about animals who are real yet metaphorically symbolize an event of significance tell us a lot about the society which is being depicted. In this context, I will discuss some animal stories of Tarapada Ray. He has written a number of short stories where animals are real and yet metaphorical, symbolizing his lost childhood, which is further mapped onto a lost land, East Bengal, from where he migrated to Kolkata during his youth as a result of Partition. Both the lost childhood and the lost land stand for purity and simplicity in Tarapada Ray's stories. Animals that were lost in his past life return repeatedly in these stories. His own topophilia is shared by the remembered animals of his childhood. This results in a deep nostalgic melancholia and also reveals the unreason of riots and Partition.

'Dudhraj' is about a snake-charmer's cobra in the crowded street of Calcutta, which reminds the author of the *bastusap* (household snake) Dudhraj (meaning as white as milk) of his childhood home. This snake never harmed anyone; in fact, it saved his family from thieves and dacoits. It had been living with them for many generations. As the family left the house for West Bengal, the snake too left with them. It followed their bullock cart till the District Board Road and then entered a bush, from where perhaps its ancestor had once come to become a *bastusap* in the author's house.

Similarly, 'Babhrubahan' describes a visit to his native village after many years. The author meets a donkey that climbs the stairs to the roof of the house, reminding him of another such donkey of his childhood, whose name was Babhrubahan.

'Sindure Megh' is about a calf that had once witnessed a house catching fire. Though the event did not cause much harm at the time. Later, when a riot in 1950 led to arson in the neighbourhood, the calf was terribly scared and ran away, never to be found again. Soon afterwards, the author's family had to leave the village.

A similar story is 'Jacob', about the author's grandfather's slightly lame horse. Jacob was a regular visitor to the verandah that was attached to the kitchen, especially when Ajima, the author's father's widowed aunt, used to cut vegetables. She would feed the horse with the peels. But Jacob 'did not have the sense of death'. One day Ajima died and Jacob followed everyone to the crematorium and saw her being cremated. Even after this, he would go to the kitchen in the hope of being fed. Tarapada is not keen to establish the intelligence of his animals; he also never translates their language for readers. To him they are creatures just like him. Jacob eats, forms habits (like Babhrubahan's habit of walking on the roof), guards the house like a dog, does not tolerate dogs and cats, but somehow recognizes and accepts the clients of his lawyer master, as well as peons and newspaper vendors. It looks for a shelter when it rains; and when it realizes that the family does not like it taking shelter in the kitchen balcony, it goes to the office verandah for shelter. Jacob is also presented as a sort of debauch—he is fascinated not by mares, but by women.

After Partition, members of the family leave for West Bengal and decide to take Jacob with them. When they go to the local Kali temple to pay obeisance to the goddess before leaving, Jacob accompanies them. However, the horse cannot be taken to India. It is detained at the border and the security forces falsely charge the family of stealing the horse. Since then, Jacob roams near the border. The author and his family see him several times, while crossing the border. Jacob used to come forward to meet them and kept looking at them with his 'unfathomably deep black eyes'. The animals, in their pure innocence, make Partition seem absolutely meaningless and cruel in Tarapada's stories.

Not all of Tarapada's animal stories are related to Partition. However, all of them relate to a lost innocent world that he experienced in his childhood. Another such tale is 'Kalukak', where the protagonist is a blind crow, who was rescued by the author's grandmother and kept as a pet. One day, he was stolen, as someone claimed that this crow was able to predict future, which made it seem valuable.

In the story 'Bishu', the protagonist is a pet cow, who was also lost to its family. One day the author and his brother found her among many other cows and goats on a *paikars*' boat. They called her and she responded, but the *paikars* refused to give her away.

Sharing a World with Animals

There are many more stories about human–animal relationships in Bengali literature. A complete survey is neither possible here nor is it my intention. Still, it is possible for us to summarize a few stories about animals who are endowed with love and intelligence not very different from humans.

'Ganesh-Janani' by Banaphul is a pleasant story. There is no cruelty here, only love. A couple with a moderate income, who own about 100 bighas of land and live in a three-room house, receive a baby elephant as a gift and keep him as their pet. They are issueless and the elephant, Ganesh, is like their son. They broaden all the doors of their house as well as two rooms for Ganesh to move about freely. They themselves occupy as little space as possible. The story is narrated by a veterinary doctor whom they call to treat Ganesh, as the latter had stopped eating. The man tells the doctor, 'When my wife goes to take her bath, Ganesh accompanies her swinging the bucket and the towel from his trunk. When she cooks in the kitchen in the heat of summer, Ganesh fans her with a hand-fan.' 'Does he understand what you say?', the doctor asks. The man answers, 'Everything! He is a veritable human. He even sulks when his feelings are hurt. I believe this the reason behind his starving now.' Earlier, Ganesh had eaten 200 mangoes from their garden kept in a basket, in their absence; and hence the woman (referred to as 'Ganesh-Janani' or 'mother of Ganesh') had slapped him on the head lightly and rebuked him. The man suspects that this has hurt Ganesh and that there is nothing physically wrong with him. This is also confirmed by the veterinary doctor. He is so moved by the couple's love for this elephant and their struggle to keep him despite their poverty that he refuses to accept any fees. At the time of his departure, he realizes that his fees have been arranged by mortgaging the lady's ornaments.

'Porarmukhi' by Sailajananda Mukhopadhyay is about a cat that almost forced a childless couple to adopt her. The couple often talk of banishing it from the house, but refrain from doing after remembering the homing instinct of cats. However, it was likely that they had really come to love her. They call her Porarmukhi, literally meaning 'one with a burnt face'. Porarmukhi gives birth to a black kitten. The lady of the house (i.e. the narrator's wife) is superstitious and believes that black cats bring bad luck. Thus, she forces her husband to leave the kitten on the road outside. But Porarmukhi brings it back in no time. Then the kitten is left at a faraway place. Proramukhi searches for it everywhere in the house and grieves pathetically. She even stops eating and meows continuously. The next morning the husband, urged by his wife, goes in search of the kitten. Meanwhile Porarmukhi too tries to find her kitten and gets run over by a car. The husband sees this and rescues her. Though she is alive, one of her legs is badly damaged. The couple attend to her wound, which, to their relief, does not seem to be very serious. Adding to their relief, the kitten soon returns on her own. The wife is delighted and, laying the kitten near its mother, says, 'Oh, yesterday she cried herself and made me cry equally. Here is your Khokan (baby), mother!' The love of a mother cat for her kitten, of a young woman (and a man) for a cat, as well as the love between a husband and a wife are treated on par in this story to reveal love as something basic in life and the world and as something that is shared between animals and humans.

'Chirikdas' by Saradindu Bandyopadhya is about a squirrel who took shelter in the author's house during a great flood in Pune. It became attached to the author's wife, was fed by her and was provided with a cage to sleep at night. But the woman's friends warned her that squirrels cannot be domesticated. Indeed, as Chirikdas grew up and felt the need for a female companion, he ran away from the house, to the sorrow and anxieties of the couple. However, after a few days' gap, the squirrel started returning home every afternoon for tea and biscuits. Just like humans, he had developed an addiction for tea. He would drink the tea, eat half the biscuit, and leave with the other half, most probably for his mate.

'Marco' by Shachindranath Bandyopadhyay is about a monkey. The author works for a paint company. He is posted at Vishakhapattanam and paints ships from all over the world. One day, a Greek sailor gives him an Australian monkey named Marco. The monkey and the author living alone away from his family become very close. Marco lightly passes his hand through the hair of the author when the latter relaxes. Marco also lies down beside the author—if the latter lies on his back, Marco does that too; if he turns on his side, Marco emulates him. When he writes and his pen runs out of ink, a keenly observant Marco comes running with the ink pot. The servant even teaches Marco to carry the tea tray.

However, during the summer vacation the author's mother and siblings come to visit him and they do not like Marco. The author temporarily gives him to an acquaintance. A heartbroken Marco starves himself to death. When the author comes to know this, it is too late. The story ends with the following lines:

How could that creature of a far off land come to love me so? Or is it the nature of love—that it is indiscriminate, that it overflows on its own like waves? Perhaps, yes. Otherwise how can the song of love resound through plants and leaves, from creature to creature, from molecules to molecules without any reason?

Manjil Sen's 'Goda' is about the friendship between a small boy, Antu, vacationing in Madhupur and a monkey who he names Goda (meaning leader of a group), because the latter was obviously the leader of a group of monkeys. Their first encounter scares Antu. Goda does not like Antu's intrusion in the garden as the latter evidently wants to pluck ripe guavas. Then, gradually a give-and-take develops. Goda takes bananas from Antu and gives him guavas in return.

Goda saves Antu from other monkeys as well as from two thieves in a desolate area in the evening. Then comes the day to say goodbye. Goda makes a sad sound and his eyes well up with tears.

It is possible that the author misinterprets the monkeys' gestures—Goda seems amused when Antu's sister is scared of him. Goda smiles when Antu offers him *telebhaja* (a fried snack). We know that when monkeys bare their teeth, it does not suggest a smile but aggression or fear. To make Goda seem more human-like, the story also stresses the athletic quality of Goda, who can catch two ripe guavas like a veteran sportsman. We have already noted how anthropomorphism regarding animals can be misleading sometimes, though overall it is perhaps better that anthropo-denial.

The way our domestic cats and dogs can befriend us and make us adopt them in the first place, express gratitude to us, and understand what sort of habits we want them to form, makes them seem very close, perhaps even superior, to humans in their intelligence and understanding. One is reminded of 'Jhunumasir Beral' by Sunil Gangopadhyay. When Jhunumasi tries to drive away a stray kitten, the latter impresses her by doing various tricks. Jhunumasi asks her servant to give the kitten a pot of milk before leaving her on the footpath. But after drinking the milk, the way the kitten gestures to thank her, melts Jhunumasi's heart and she keeps the kitten as a pet, naming her Flossy. But confusions and contradictions within humans regarding animals are revealed once again in this story. Tunimasi, who hates cats, visits Jhunumasi one day and drives Flossy away. Jhunumasi is heartbroken.

An advertisement is put up and a reward announced for anyone who found her. Many people arrive with cats, though of course, Jhunumasi only wants Flossy. Those who come with cats do not bother to take them back and leave them at her place. Then one day, Flossy returns on her own, as is the wont of cats, a talent humans do not recognize as intelligence. Jhunumasi keeps all the cats as her pets. Her loving accommodation is extended from one cat to many.

'Nyadosh' by Mahashweta Devi, another humorous story, narrates the tale of a cow who destroys everything at home (books, clothes, etc.), has a preference for blue, is a non-vegetarian (she especially likes hilsa and chicken) ,and can climb stairs. Her preference for blue or hilsa may not be realistic, but humanizes her. An account of her driving police constables into the river Ganga by waving her horns as well as the filing of police cases against her ('Nyadosh was perhaps the only cow of the British regime against whom a number of police cases were filed') adds to this humanization.

'Himachaler Swapna' by Hemendra Kumar Roy is about a bear born in the Himalayas and then captured and sold to a man who used to entertain people, children in particular, by making animals dance and perform tricks. After the man's death, the bear was shifted to a small cage in the Alipore Zoo. The author describes the bear's urge to dance and his craving for the freedom he once enjoyed in the Himalayas. One day, the bear escaped from the zoo and went on an adventure, terrorizing humans despite his innocence and, at the same time, winning the hearts of children. This story is clearly meant for children. While the bear is adorable, he is perhaps too anthropomorphic. However, the story is surely capable of sensitizing children to animals, their sorrows and happiness. It also implies that human incapability lies behind their failure to understand animals.[25]

Yet, a Gap Remains

Despite deep human–animal mutuality and love, sometimes the gap cannot be bridged fully, howsoever bad human beings might feel about this. This applies particularly to wild creatures (corroborating the concept of 'otherwild').

Although wild creatures can sometimes be domesticated, they remain somewhat strange and distant from human society. This is revealed in the story 'Jimmy' by Syed Mustafa Siraj. Jimmy is an otter whose mother was killed by a python. The author, who witnessed the incident, liked the way the baby otter tried to help his mother during the fight ('I liked the baby's devotion to his mother and his desperation'), took pity on the orphan , and brought it home. It became his pet, was civilized and friendly with the author's dog, Jacky. After some time, however, Jimmy started leaving the house at night and bringing home a variety of fishes. His otter's instinct was activated. One day he returns with blood stains all over his body. The author is horrified. However, he soon finds that the blood is not Jimmy's, but somebody else's. It is discovered that Jimmy has killed that python and thus avenged his mother's death. After accomplishing this, the otter seems to smile in satisfaction.

That Jimmy is not an ordinary, domestic animal is stressed throughout the story. Yet the tale makes the otter seem perhaps too human-like—not only avenging his mother's death and smiling triumphantly, but also in the way the author translates his gestures into words. When the author tries to dry Jimmy with a towel after his first night's adventure, Jimmy seems to say, 'Oh, leave it. We are used to be in water at night. Don't you worry for this'. Jacky's gestures are also similarly interpreted. When the author rebukes Jacky for letting Jimmy leave the house at night, Jacky seems to repent. The author writes, 'He looks on sadly. He evidently did not realize the implication of this before.'

Occasionally, when a wild animal is domesticated, its human friends have to bid it farewell eventually. 'Akash-Patal', a story by Geeta Bandyopadhyay depicts one such instance. The children of a family that loves hunting bring home a baby crane, found alive among a pile of dead ducks. It had seemingly come to Delhi in the winter as part of a group of migratory birds from Siberia. Though at first one of the hunters wants to kill it, the others object. Gradually everyone comes to love the crane, named Bokuram. Its behaviour is amusing as well. When summer comes and it feels the heat, it would enter the washroom with its long legs and soak its wings with water. Then it would take the author's towel from the clothes stand and start drying itself. After this, it would lightly brush the author's face with that towel and rub the snout of the cat with it as well, by way of teasing them, and then put the towel back on the stand. This would, of course, bring down the roof with laughter. But one day, the bird shows signs of restlessness. Migratory birds were beginning to return home. One, two, three groups fly across the sky. Bokuram flies away with the third group, leaving its human friends forlorn.

Geeta Bandyopadhyay's short novel 'Bobby-r Bandhu' is a classic narrative of taming a wild animal and then bidding it farewell. In this case, however, it is not the animal's natural instinct but an unnatural and violent man-made situation that leads to this heart-wrenching moment of parting.

The novel is set in Mandalay, Burma, just before the Second World War. A motherless little girl, Mini, lives there with her elder sister and brother-in-law. The latter is an animal-lover and so the house is like a menagerie, with fourteen dogs, three cats, two rabbits, one monkey, two parrots and quite a few chickens living there. Preparations for the coming war could be felt all around, but there is no sense of anxiety among the people yet. At least this Bengali family and those associated with it (a next-door neighbor named Jefferson, also a number of local Burmese people) were still not bothered. One day, the family goes on a hunting trip to a nearby forest and brings home a baby bear whose mother had been killed the day before. The bear resents its capture and proves extremely difficult to tame. But Mini takes an immediate liking to it, names it Bobby and insists on adopting it. She is badly scratched and injured by the bear quite a few times but does not relent. Ultimately, the bear and the girl develop a sense of interdependency and become deeply attached to each other. Bobby accepts the animals of the house as well and is accepted by them in return. But his wild nature shows itself every now and then and the human adults believe him to be dangerous. They want to sell him, but Mini resists such attempts.

The entire story is fun-filled, as it describes a variety of animal and human characters, their habits and behaviours as well as their relationships with one another, as seen through the eyes of the little girl. Symbiosis and harmony is stressed above jealousy and conflicts. But this happy situation was increasingly disturbed by the approaching war. Blackouts and sirens became part of daily life. Then one day there was continuous bombing, causing panic among humans and animals alike. The bombing killed a local man, who was the father of a close friend of Mini. The entire city was burning. The family could not abandon their animals and took shelter in the trenches. They realized that they would have to make a hard decision. They gave a few dogs to their next-door neighbour Jefferson and prepared to leave the rest of the animals, including Bobby, in the jungle before leaving the place themselves. The animals were, however, reluctant to leave. At first, the parrot cage was opened. The birds took a few steps out of the open door, but then went back inside. Even the adults were in tears upon seeing this.

A big cage-like car was constructed to take the other animals to the jungle. Jefferson and his servant Abdul, both of whom were close to the family and particularly fond of Mini, accompanied the family on this trip. But on reaching the edge of the jungle no animal would leave the car. They started howling and had to be forced out. At last, it was Bobby's turn, the wildest of them all. But Bobby stood his ground and would not move. Mini's brother-in-law asked Mini to hold his leash, take him to the jungle and leave him there, because the bear would only obey her. Before this moment, Mini did not have the heart to look at the animals, including Bobby. But now she had to obey her brother-in-law. With Mini calling her, Bobby agreed to go into the jungle. He looked enthusiastic and started dragging her forward. However, after they reached the jungle and Mini asked Bobby to leave, he would not obey, nor would he let her go. Abdul, who loved both Mini and Bobby, came forward to take charge of the situation. Mini handed over Bobby's leash to Abdul and ran back to the car with tears running down her cheeks. After the car started, Abdul ran back and got in. Bobby now started running desperately, following the car. He almost managed to catch up with them. Mini's brother-in-law asked Jefferson to shoot Bobby. As Jefferson took aim with his pistol, Mini made an impassioned plea, 'Na, na, na . . .'. Abdul jumped out of the car, stopped his master, and assured Mini that he would look after Bobby. Mini felt grateful. But,

Seeing Abdul come running towards him, Bobby suddenly stopped and thought for a moment. Then he raised both his hands towards the sky, cried out and started running towards the jungle. My golden chain that I had made him wear, dazzled on his neck. Abdul started running after him. But both of them disappeared from our view before we could understand whether Abdul was able to catch him or not.

The conclusion of the story, particularly Bobby throwing his hands towards the sky and his human well-wishers' heartache about the uncertainty of his destiny, seems to be a metaphor for the ultimate uncertainty in human–animal relationships. This story concludes my attempt to understand this indecisive relationship with the help of Bengali literature. Let us, however, try to write an inconclusive conclusion!

Conclusion

Postcolonial scholars often argue that the fundamental predicament of studying non-humans is that it must happen through 'monohumanism', i.e. constructing the world in human terms and ignoring alternative politico-cultural formations.[26] 'Monohumanism' is close to what we have called 'anthropocentricism'. Postcolonial critics argue that because the minds of animals remain elusive to us, all we can do is to study the process in which the animal is made the dialectical other vis-à-vis the human identity. Moreover, for these scholars, monohumanism is associated with the Western ideology of secular liberalism that has elevated the white, European male in human reckoning. Thus, to avoid falling in the trap of monohumanism, they study the discursive appropriation of animals for dominating racial, colonized, gendered and disabled others in the modern period, showing the entanglement of such forms of oppression and blaming this mostly on colonialism and its related forces. Indeed, as we have noted in the previous chapter, scholars like Michael Lundblad think that one should engage with 'animality studies rather than "animal studies"'. Postcolonial literary critics, hence, are not interested in the portrayal of 'real' animals in literature and dismiss the attitude of liking or romanticizing them.

Postcolonial zoocriticism examines representations of animals within colonialism and its legacy; they try to uncover in literature the ways in which imperialism (and later successor states) used animals to dehumanize the colonized and how the latter used animals to protest against that dehumanizing process. To show the views of the colonized, they usually consider literary works written comparatively recently, which are perhaps consciously postcolonial in their approach.

Let us consider *Postcolonial Animalities*, edited by Suvadip Sinha and Amit R. Baishya, which is an important recent contribution to postcolonial literary studies.[27] It upholds Lundblad's approach and is about 'imaginaries of the human with grammars of animality', but at the same time it claims to somewhat differ from Lundblad by showing concern for real animals, in both their 'materialist and representational renditions', their agency and alterity. The book largely conforms to postcolonial zoocriticism by seeking to rewrite the biopolitical story of both humanity and animality. It avowedly seeks to show 'animalities' as 'a series of shifting relational terrains that move in and out of the human and nonhuman'.

The few examples from Bengali literature used in the book, however, feature metaphorical versions of animals only. Gautam Basu Thakur discusses Mahashweta Devi's story on pterodactyls ('Pterodactyl, Puran Sahay and Pirtha')[28] and Sinha studies Nabarun Bhattacharya's novella *Lubdhak*.[29] Basu Thakur, in his article, uses literary works that present 'animals whose excessive otherness disrupts the human as the subject-supposed-to-know'. Mahashweta Devi herself said that she had used the pterodactyl as a symbol for the suffering tribal people, while Gayatri Spivak, who translated the story into English, interpreted the extinct animal reappearing in the contemporary period as a metaphor for the impossibility of representing the subaltern. Yet, Basu Thakur argues that the creature seems real because it 'exists as alterity underived from the human, manifests the radical antagonism constitutive of human (non)relation to the animal'. One thing is, however, certain—the creature is a metaphor either way, despite Basu Thakur's roundabout claim regarding its reality.[30]

In the novella *Lubdhak*, a plan to get rid of the street dogs of Kolkata creates an atmosphere of terror and precarity. However, this is an allegory for human vulnerability, since humans with low socio-economic status were becoming increasingly animalized and hence being considered disposable. Bhattacharya somewhat anthropomorphizes the dogs and shows their ontological mutuality with humans. The dogs also protest and claim their agency by voluntarily staging an exodus from the city under the instruction of their cosmic counterpart, the Dog Star (Canis Minor), who would send an asteroid to destroy the city soon. Thus, they challenge the speciesist illusion of the human lifeworld and remind the humans of their zoopolitical vulnerability. Sinha claims reality for the dogs portrayed in the novel—a reality which lies not in their anthropomorphization but in their barks that permeate the novel alongside their human-like speech, thus inverting the human claim of superiority based on language. However, despite this claim, the dogs in the novella are actually metaphorical and not real! On the other hand, even if we accept that perhaps the reality of literary representations of animals remains a matter of degree, does that not also apply to literary representations of humans?

It is this doubt that makes my study of animals in Bengali literature different from postcolonial studies. While I am fascinated by the concept of `animality', in this book I am more interested in flesh-and-blood animals and I wanted to find how close literature could come to their interiority by challenging 'monohumanism'.[31] There is another vital point of difference. I tend to understand human history from the perspective of 'deep history', which merges human history with the history of life, and which is, methodologically speaking, neuro-history. Deep history tries to understand human beings in terms of human nature embedded in brain and body chemistry. If we adopt this perspective, we cannot start understanding history from the modern period, which many postcolonial scholars do. Particularly, the focus of my interest—human–animal relationship—is a subject that has to be studied in the context of a deep past and in terms of human nature.[32] Considering this history (also even history of 'animality') from the time of the Enlightenment and colonial expansion somewhat flattens and foreshortens the narrative.

In my study of Bengali literature, I have considered stories written only from the late nineteenth century onwards (I wish I could look further backward, but there are not enough materials). Of course, the stories have specific social settings, which are important for them. But they also tend to transcend those settings by portraying the central human and animal characters as individual members of universal species that throb with life, form attachment, struggle to survive, and so on. Thus, the stories feature real, rather than metaphorical, animals and their relationships with humans; though at the same time animals as metaphors for dominance-hierarchies in the human order lurk in many of the stories, revealing emotions like envy, hatred, aggression, violence, protest, love and, above all, 'animality' in human nature. The stories are desperate attempts to retain the human urge to empathize with and love animals, sometimes at the risk of romanticizing the latter; they also often agonize over the limitations of such urges. My reading of the stories may be considered as an extension of 'animal studies'.

A standard critique of such stories of human-animal relationships is that of anthropomorphism as well as anthropocentrism.[33] It is said that the writers tend to humanize animals and actually think of humans while writing the stories. The animals portrayed in them are nothing other than what the writers make them. It has also been shown by critics that perceiving human traits in animals may be wrong, that human interpretations of animal behaviour can well be misinterpretations. Such humanization also tends to be too sentimental. It has even been said that the writers are actually reinforcing the domination of man, for the animals in these stories, more often than not, internalize their loyalty to man as natural, which may not be the reality. Ultimately man is presented as the master in these stories. Another criticism is that the writers of animal stories are selective, they convert only some select non-moral objects as metonymical to moral subjects. They show concern for only some individual animals that some individual humans find significant, thus turning them into moral subjects from their own human point of view.

Perhaps the animal stories discussed above do also have the above limitations. Eventually, however, the critics cannot take much away from the stories. It is evident that to write animal stories without including aspects of anthropomorphism and anthropocentricism is almost impossible. However, unlike the anthropomorphism and anthropocentrism associated with laboratory experimentation, xenotransplantation, etc., which turns subjects into objects, writers of animal stories turn objects into subjects. They do this by stressing on our common physicality, somatic needs, bodily sufferings as well as commonalities in our mental processes. Today, animal studies scholars are countering the Cartesian logic 'I think therefore I am' with Derrida's 'the animal therefore I am', and the latter seems to be a more valid proposition. At least the story writers thought so. Some of the stories thus reveal the animality of humans too—hunger, sexuality etc. The writers try to imply that the fate of all living beings is decided by biological imperatives rather than any higher transcendental principle; this also includes emotions. Emotion as well as intelligence of animals is stressed in these stories, which closes the gap between humans and animals. It is important that the writers claim for animals not only a representational space but also a moral space by turning them into moral subjects. Regarding the charge that they are selective in their moral feelings for animals, it can be argued that selectiveness is inevitable in any ethic of care. It is only natural and practical to limit the scope of our individual concerns to certain creatures over others, and to privilege certain relationships over others, as Dolgert has pointed out. But perhaps a kind of moral generalization, too, emerges here. We have moreover seen that even wild animals and animals used for meat have drawn the writers' empathy in some cases. All the stories cry out powerfully—'Treat them as fellow creatures', 'They have something more than mere use-values.' This moral message goes beyond concern for an individual animal and embraces the entire animal world in a way. But of course, the writers never make any overt moral or political claim on their behalf; rather, they show how love and morality is often defeated in real life. However, it is precisely by foregrounding sorrow and despair that they seem to plead for better treatment of animals.

The stories present the possibility of a strong bond and love between humans and animals—love that is no less emotive and noble than that between two human beings. A dog can be closer to a man than his own spouse (i.e. as in the story 'Jantab'). This challenges the real world, where animals are either slaves or objects to eat or experiment with, or mere 'environment' lurking in the background, or practically invisible (in fact, this is why we easily use them as food, clothing or laboratory objects). These stories place animals centre stage and make them visible in their relationship with man. They try to denaturalize the way humans have always thought about animals. This seems to be their greatest achievement.[34]

If the stories have problems in fully comprehending animals and in perfectly representing them, if they privilege some animals over others, if ultimately humans seem to be the masters—these are problems found in most human stories, and, indeed, in real life as well. Are we not biased towards some humans against others? Do we not become oppressive to some humans by simply making them invisible? Most of us never experience or truly engage with the reality of the sufferings and death of animals, which is true also of our relationships with poor farmers, who can thus be easily evicted from their lands for the sake of 'development', whose desperate suicide cannot really perturb us. Also, do we often not want to be the dominant partner in a relationship? Can humans understand each other fully? Is there not a communication gap even between humans apparently very close to each other? Are we not like islands trying to empathize, to reach out, but never fully succeeding? Also, do we not often find our language inadequate for expressing our deepest thoughts, particularly on relationships? Still isn't human life all about our striving to overcome or get around these problems, even though we may seldom succeed?

Notes

1. *Tuntunir Boi* was first published in 1911. Numerous editions were published later.
2. For Victorians, the crocodile was a potent symbol of the colonized or racial other, and had powerful associations with exoticism and Orientalism. The crocodile became a key nineteenth-century imperialist symbol after Napoleon's invasion of Egypt in 1798. The British deployed the crocodile as a symbol for Napoleon himself, stressing its association with his insatiable appetite. See Mary Elizabeth Leighton and Lisa Surridge, 'The Empire Bites Back: The Racialized

Crocodile of the Nineteenth Century', in *Victorian Animal Dreams: Representations of Animals in Victorian Literature and Culture*, ed. Martin A. Danahay and Deborah Denenholz Morse, Ashgate, England and Burlington, USA: Routledge, 2007.

3. The Romantics emphasized the need to treat animal life with more respect. They composed elegies for deceased pets (e.g. Lord Byron's epitaph for his dog Boatswain in 1808 with the epitaph: 'All the virtues of man without his vices'), lamented exploitation of work animals (e.g. Samuel Taylor Coleridge's 'To a Young Ass'), urged readers to consider even the rights of insects (e.g. William Blake's 'The Fly'), criticized the sadistic pleasure of hunting (e.g. William Wordsworth's 'Hart-Leap Well'), and published pamphlets promoting vegetarianism (e.g. P.B. Shelley's 'A Vindication of Natural Diet'). The radical liberal politics that was criticizing man's exploitative nature, particularly the dehumanizing labour conditions, was also associated with this pro-animal attitude.

4. The horse in Tarapada Ray's story 'Babhrubahan', where the protagonist is a donkey who climbs the stairs to the roof of the house, Ray's 'Jacob' who is a horse and a creature of peculiar habits, Sharadindu Bandyopadhyay's 'Chirikdas', a squirrel who develops an addiction for tea, and Mahashweta Devi's 'Nyadosh', a cow who had preference for the color blue and for hilsa fish. These stories will be discussed in more detail later.

5. Prabhat Mukhopadhyay's 'Adarini', an elephant, or Tarasankar Bandyopadhyay's 'Kalapahar', an ox—both stories end in a tragedy.

6. Saratchandra Chattopadhyay's 'Mahesh' and Narayan Gangopadhyay's 'Jantab', respectively.

7. Tarasankar Bandyopadhyay's 'Nari o Nagini' and 'Kamdhenu', respectively.

8.   Tarasankar Bandyopadhyay's 'Kalapahar', the ox, who stands with his feet cemented to the ground so that nobody can move him against his wishes.

9.   Dibyendu Palit's 'Bhuli', where the protagonist is a dog, or Manjil Sen's 'Goda', a monkey.

10. In Sharatchandra's 'Mahesh', the bull's sufferings are intertwined with the sufferings of his master, Gafur, who is a poor peasant and a Muslim, helpless in the face of his Hindu superiors. In Abul Bashar's 'Harbola's Dak', inspired by 'Mahesh', poverty minus the religious dimension is portrayed. In Rameshchandra Sen's 'Sada Ghora', the Partition riots endanger the lives of both the horse and its poor Muslim syce, and eventually, even though the syce can be saved, the horse dies.

11. Shailajanda Mukhopadhyay's story 'Kala', about a deaf dog.

12. Stefan Dolgert, 'Species of Disability: Response to Arneil', *Political Theory*, December 2010. Here he responds to Barbara Arneil, 'Disability, Self-image and Modern Political Theory', *Political Theory*, April 2009. We have discussed Dolgert's views in the first chapter.

13. Tarasankar Bandyopadhyay's 'Doggie: Alsatian Noy' and 'Suku o Bhuku', Dibyendu Palit's 'Bhuli', Leela Majumdar's 'Bhow Bhow Yap Yap' are all stories of dogs. In Geeta Bandyopadhyay's novel *Bobby-r Bandhu*, meaning 'Bobby's friend', the friend of the bear named Bobby is a little girl who keeps him against the wishes of her adult guardians. In Bibhutibhushan's 'Budhir Bari Phera' it is the little girl of the house who loves the cow most. In Hemendranath Ray's 'Himachaler Swapna', the bear discovers a 'great truth' from his experiences as a dancing bear and his life in the zoo—that no one can love him more than human kids.

14. Manjil Sen's 'Goda' and Leela Majumdar's 'Bhow Bhow Yap Yap'.
15. 'Kala', where the protagonist is a disabled dog.
16. For example, 'Doggie: Alsatian Noy'.
17. 'Bhuli', 'Kala', and 'Goda'.
18. Sharadindu Bandyopadhya's 'Pintu'.
19. We will not discuss the aesthetic view of the authors separately. In animal stories aesthetics is rooted in ethics or, rather, in love. The animal's appearance is described in a way that inspires sentiments of tenderness and love. After all, whether aesthetics is subjectivist and ahistorical or whether it is inspired by a practical rationality rooted in reality, there is always a close relationship between beauty and love. See Peter Heymans, *Animality in British Romanticism: The Aesthetics of Species*, New York: Routledge, London.
20. The agrarian culture of north India also produced such stories. Draught animals feature prominently in some of Premchand's stories. 'The Story of Two Bullocks' and other stories can be cited. See Premchand, *Stories on Animals*, ed. M. Asauddin, Penguin Viking, 2018.
21. Pradyumna Bhattacharya, 'Natun Jatak?', *Sahitya Parishat Patrika* (Tarasankar Shatatama Jayanti Sankalan), Kolkata: Bangiya Sahitya Parishat, 1999.
22. Bhattacharya uses Pascal to understand this.
23. Michelle Superle, while reviewing English dog stories, notices this pattern too. He calls such stories mythological, because they are sort of creation myths, signifying a rebirth. They present heroic beings (in this case, dogs) as superior to ordinary humans and facilitate a breakthrough of the 'sacred' in the form of nature, wildness and childhood. See Michelle Superle, 'Animal Heroes and Transforming Substances: Canine Characters in Contemporary Children's Literature', in *Animals and the Human Imagination: A Companion*

to *Animal Studies*, ed. Aaron Gross and Anne Vallely, New York: Columbia University Press, 2012.

24. There is another kind of 'disability' in Indian society. As in the case of animals, this too is an embodied prejudice and practice. It is untouchability rooted in the caste system. Empathy and sympathy between an untouchable person and an animal can come naturally. While I have not found any story in Bengali literature portraying such relationship, Premchand wrote 'The Price of Milk', where an orphan Bhangi boy with no one to care for him becomes attached to a dog: 'If there was someone he could call his own, it was a pariah dog of the village who tired of being picked on by his fellow dogs, has taken refuge with him.' See Premchand, *Stories on Animals*.

25. There are more such animals in Bengali literature. They present animals who are perhaps a bit too anthropomorphic and yet retain their basic species entities as cats, dogs, foxes and so on, and seek to win the child reader's heart. Shibani Raychaudhury's books for children, featuring Mashgul, the cat, Hyanglacharan, the street dog, etc., are some recent examples. See *Mashgul*, Kolkata: Thema, 2018; *Bejarmukho Raghabboyal*, Kolkata: Thema, 2019.

26. Sylvia Wynter, Introduction to *Postcolonial Animalities*, ed. Suvadp Sinha and Amit R. Baishya, New York and Oxfordshire: Routledge, 2020, p. 6.

27. Ibid.

28. Gautam Basu Thakur, '"A Strangeness beyond Reckoning": The Animal as Surplus in Postcolonial Literature', in *Postcolonial Animalities*, ed. Sinha and Baishay. The author has used Mahashweta Devi, 'Pterodactyl, Puran Sahay and Pirtha', in *Imaginary Maps*, tr. Gayatri Chakraborty Spivak, New York and Oxfordshire: Routledge, 1994.

29. Suvadip Sinha, 'Pariah Dogs: Precarious Cohabiation', in *Postcolonial Animalities*. He has used Nabarun

Bhattacharya, *Lubdhak*, included in *Upanyas Samagra*, Kolkata: Dey's Publishing, 2010.

30. Basu Thakur also discusses in this article Amitav Ghosh's novel *Hungry Tide*, which presents the ethical conundrum of whether to side with refugees seeking resettlement in the archipelago of Sundarbans or whether to preserve the area for the endangered Royal Bengal tigers. That supporting the refugees would harm the deltaic islands' ecosystem is clear. The novelist seeks a way out by portraying human–animal 'symbiotic codependency' and advocating 'culture-specific location-based environmentalism'.

    However, Basu Thakur points out how usually the reading of the novel 'overlooks the animals that are irreducible to matters of symbiotic politics and knowledge constitution'. He highlights the crabs that 'scrawl all over the narrative', who are the custodians and architects of the deltaic islands, who keep the mangroves alive by removing their leaves and litter. The crabs are also a rich source of nutrients for poor humans. But they aggressively challenge the human efforts to mould their natural environment by constantly burrowing into the man-made dykes. They are so small and apparently insignificant creatures that they also escape human knowledge-power system just like the extinct animal pterodactyl. Thus, in the novel, crabs help portray nature as a primal world—indifferent, asocial, brutal, and beyond redemption. Thus, Basu Thakur points to the impossibility of a satisfactory resolution of the moral debate, which in the novel leads to an advocacy of symbiotic politics as far as humans and the tigers are concerned. He argues that the crabs present the real dilemma of *Hungry Tide*—the dilemma of how to balance human need with nature, or 'the impossibility of achieving balance with nature being human'.

31. Presenting metaphorical animals cannot really achieve this, even if a writer totally inverts the usual relationship of domination and subordination between humans and animals. Under the impact of posthumanism and postcolonialism, varieties of animal stories are being written in English. There are even stories that do not even acknowledge human presence or create a situation where non-human animals are in a more advantageous position than humans. In Yann Martel's novel *Life of Pi*, in an inversion of the reader's ready expectation, the tiger has a family name and the human is denoted by a symbol (Pi). The tiger and the man find themselves in a lifeboat on the Pacific after their ship sinks. The tiger can adapt to the situation more easily by eating flying fish, etc., which Pi cannot initially, though gradually he learns to do this. He also learns to control the tiger, but only by acknowledging and re-inhabiting his own animality. We are also reminded of Will Self's *Great Apes*, where apes live in houses, have jobs, families, etc., while humans live in cages. 'They are so cute', remarks one chimp visitor to the human zoo. In this narrative, primatology becomes anthropology, a branch of zoology. And a primate anthropologist tries to interpret human language. The difference is thus collapsed. I have not come across such total inversions in Bengali literature, which would have been appreciated by postcolonial critics.

32. Perhaps from the time when humans lived by hunting members of other species, as well as befriending and domesticating some of them, when they massacred the entire species of Neanderthals who were actually not much different physically or in terms of material culture. What is more interesting is that *Homo sapiens* massacred the Neanderthals with the help of yet another species, more distant in evolutionary

terms, i.e. their dogs. For what *Homo sapiens* did to the Neanderthals see Pat Shipman, *The Invaders: How Humans and Their Dogs Drove Neanderthals to Extinction*, Cambridge: Harvard University Press, 2015; see also Thomas R. Trautmann, Gillian Feeley-Harnik and John C. Mitani, 'Deep Kinship', in *Deep History: The Architecture of Past and Present*, ed. Daniel Lord Smail and Andrew Shryock, Berkeley and London: University of California, 2011.

33.   Both animal studies and literary studies of animal fictions are new academic areas in India. We do not find such criticism in the context of Bengal. I am mostly referring to criticism in connection with English stories.

34.   Hence, sometimes the human order can feel threatened by such stories. Narayan Gangopadhyaya's 'Lal Ghora' is a story about a child's attraction for his father's horse, who was poisoned by hostile people, went berserk and had to be killed. This story was once included in the Class VI Bengali textbook of Bangladesh, but removed in 2016 under the pressure of Islamic organizations. It was found to be 'a conspiracy against Islamic practice of Qurbani'. See Maruf Rasul, 'Pathyapustak Paribartan: Manojagate Adhipatyabaer Rajneeti,' cited by Nilanjan Chatterjee in 'Evolution of History Curriculum and Textbooks in Bangladesh, 1947–1990', unpublished MPhil thesis, Jadavpur University, 2020. On the other hand, such stories have wide and deep appeal, have contributed to the betterment of human understanding of non-humans and put in perspective human–animal relationship.

Bibliography

Bengali Writings

Anonymous, 'Kukkur o Beral athaba Swadhinata, Swarthaparata o Premer Katha', *Bandhav*, vol. 5, no. 2, 1287/1880.

Bandyopadhyay, Bibhutibhushan, 'Budhir Bari Phera', in *Kinnardal*, Kolkata: Katyayani Book Stall, 1938.

Bandyopadhyay, Geeta, 'Akash-Patal', in *Kishore Rachana Sambhar-1*, Kolkata: Dey's Publishing, 1994.

———, 'Kukul aar Elomelo', in *Kishore Rachana Sambhar-1*, Kolkata: Dey's Publishing, 1994.

———, 'Bobby-r Bandhu', in *Kishore Rachana Sambhar-1*, Kolkata: Dey's Publishing, 1994.

Bandyopadhyay, Shachindranath, 'Marco', *Sagarika*, Kolkata: Dev Sahitya Kutir, 1971.

Bandyopadhyay, Sharadindu, 'Pintu', *Sharadindu Omnibus*, vol. 4, Kolkata: Ananda Publishers, 1974.

———, 'Chirikdas', *Sharadindu Omnibus*, vol. 7, Kolkata: Ananda Publishers, 1977.

Bandyopadhyay, Tarasankar, 'Kalapahar', *Rasakali*, Baisakh, 1345/1938.

———, 'Kamdhenu', *Kathashilpa*, 1353/1946.

———, 'Nari o Nagini', *Sharadiya Desh*, 1341/1934.

———, 'Suku o Bhuku', *Sharadiya*, 1368/1961.

———, 'Doggie: Alsatian Noy', *Jhilimili*, 1374/1967.

Bashar, Abul, 'Harbolar Dak', *Sab Galpoi Jibjantur*, ed.

Himanish Goswami, Kolkata: Pratikshan Publications, 1994.

Bhattacharya, Mahashweta (Devi), *Galper Goru Nyadosh*, Kolkata: Ankur Prakashani, n.d.

Bhattacharya, Nabarun, 'Lubdhak', *Nabarun Bhattacharya Upanyas Samagra*, Kolkata: Dey's Publishing, 2010.

Bhattacharya, Pradyumna, 'Kalapahar: Natun Jatak?', *Sahitya Parishat Patrika*, vols. 1–4, Special issue on Tarasankar Bandyopadhyay, 1999.

Chattopadhyay, Sharatchnadra, 'Mahesh', 1922; repr., *Sarat Sahitya Sangraha*, vol. 13, Kolkata: M.C. Sarkar and Sons, n.d.

Das, Jibanananda, 'Aat Bachar Ager Ekdin', *Jibananda Das-er Shreshtha Kabita*, Kolkata: Bharbi, 1954.

Devi, Jyotirmoyee, 'Putreshti', *Masik Basumati*, 1358/1951.

Gangopadhyay, Sunil, 'Jhunumasir Beral', *Beralta na Pheralta*, ed. Asok Kumar Mitra, Kolkata: Nirmal Book Agency, n.d.

Gangopadhyay, Narayan, 'Jantab', in *Narayan Gangopadhyayer Shrestha Galpo*, 7th edn., Kolkata: Prakash Bhavan, 1393/1986.

———, 'Idu Mianr Morga', in *Gandharaj*, 1362/1955, see https://www.earki.co/story/article/3601/%E0%A6% 87%E0%A6%A6%E0%A7%81-%E0%A6%AE% E0%A6%BF%E0%A6%9E%E0%A6%BE%E0%A 6%B0-%E0%A6%AE%E0%A7%8B%E0%A6%B0 %E0%A6%97%E0%A6%BE, accessed 16 February 2023.

———, 'Lal Ghora', *Galpasamagra*, vol. 2, Kolkata: Mitra o Ghosh, n.d.

Majumdar, Leela, 'Bhow Bhow Yap Yap', in *Chirakaler Galpo-Gatha*, Kolkata: Punashcha, 1991.

———, 'Manusher Galpo', in *Chirakaler Galpo-Gatha*, Kolkata: Punashcha, 1991.

———, *Chirakaler Galpo-Gatha*, Kolkata: Punashcha, 1991.

Mukhopadhaya, Bhudev, 'Pashwadi Palan', in *Paribarik Prabandha*, originally published 1882, 9th edn., 1326/1919, see https://archive.org/details/in.ernet. dli.2015.357404, accessed 16 February 2023.

Mukhopadhyay, Balaichand, 'Ganesh-Janani', in *Banaphuler Galpo-Sangraha, Dwitiya Shatak*, Kolkata: Indian Associated Publishing Company, 1970s.

Mukhopadhyay, Prabhat Kumar, 'Adarini', *Sahitya*, 1320/1913; repr. in *Prabhat Kumar Mukhopahdyayer Srestha Galpo*, 6th edn., Kolkata: Prakash Bhavan, 1389.

Mukhopadhyay, Sailajananda, 'Kala', *Mouchak*, 1342/1935.

———, 'Porarmukhi', in *Jato Kando Mao Miu*, ed. Siddhartha Ghosh, Kolkata: Subarnarekha, 2002.

Nag, Anindita, 'Wuhan To Amaderi Kirti', *Anandabazar Patrika*, 22 April 2020.

Palit, Dibyendu, 'Bhuli', in *Sab Galpoi Jibjantur*, ed. Himanish Goswami, Kolkata: Pratikshan Publications, 1994.

Ray, Tarapada, *Galpasamagra*, vol. 1, Kolkata: Mitra o Ghosh Publishers, 1995.

Raychauchuri, Upendrakishore, *Tuntunir Boi*, 1911; repr. as *Upendrakishore Rachanasamgra*, Kolkata: Reflect Publication, 2009.

Raychaudhuri, Shibani, *Bejarmukho Raghabboyal*, Kolkata: Thema, 2019.

———, *Mashgul*, Kolkata: Thema, 2018.

Roy, Hemendra Kumar, 'Himachaler Swapna', in *Hemedra Kumar Ray Rachanabali*, vol. 1, see https://bn.bdebooks.com/books/%e0%a6%b9%e0%a6%bf%e0%a6%ae%e0%a6%be%e0%a6%9a%e0%a6%b2%e0%a7%87%e0%a6%b0-%e0%a6%b8%e0%a7%8d%e0%a6%ac%e0%a6%aa%e0%a7%8d%e0%a6%a8-%e0%a6%b9%e0%a7%87%e0%a6%ae%e0%a7%87%e0%a6%a8%e0%a7%8d%e0%a6%a6/, accessed 16 February 2023.

Sen, Manjil, 'Goda', in *Sab Galpoi Jibjantur*, ed. Himanish Goswami, Kolkata: Pratikshan Publications, 1994.

Sen, Ramesh, 'Sada Ghora', *Rameshchandra Sener Srestha Galpo*, ed. Samir Ray and Samar Chanda, Kolkata: Prathamata, 1986.

Siraj, Syed Mustafa, 'Jimmy', in *Sab Galpoi Jibjantur*, ed. Himanish Goswami, Kolkata: Pratikshan Publications, 1994.

Tagore, Rabindranath, 'Anadhikar Prabesh', 1894; repr., in *Rabindra Rachanabali*, vol. 19, Kolkata: Viswa-Bharati Publications, 1968.

———, 'Praner Ras', in *Shyamali*, 1343 BS/1936, see https://rabindra-rachanabali.nltr.org/node/14284, accessed 16 February 2023.

Tagore, Balendranath, 'Pashupriti', *Chitra o Kavya*, Kolkata: Adi Brahmo Samaj, 1301/1894.

English Books and Articles

Agamben, Giorgio, *Homo Sacer: Sovereign Power and Bare Life*, Stanford: Stanford University Press, 1998.

Arneil, Barbara, 'Disability, Self-image and Modern Political Theory', *Political Theory*, vol. 37, no. 2, 2009.

———, 'Animals and Interdependence: Reply to Dolgert', *Political Theory*, vol. 38, no. 6, 2010.

Basu Thakur, Gautam, '"A Strangeness beyond Reckoning": The Animal as Surplus in Postcolonial Literature', in *Postcolonial Animalities*, ed. Suvadip Sinha and Amit R. Baishya, New York and London: Routledge, 2020.

Benston, Kimberly W., 'Experimenting at the Threshold: Sacrifice, Anthropomorphism, and the Aims of "Critical Animal Studies"', *Publications of the Modern language Association*, vol. 124, no. 2, 2009.

Bhattacharya, Mahashweta (Devi), 'Pterodactyl, Puran Sahay and Pirtha', in *Imaginary Maps: Three Stories* by *Mahashweta Devi*, tr. Gayatri Chakraborty Spivak, London: Routledge, 1994.

Chakravorti Koyeli and Madhumita Chatterjee, 'History of Speciesist Thought', *History*, 2002.

Chakrabarti, Pratik, 'Beasts of Burden: Animals and Laboratory Research in Colonial India', *History of Science*, vol. 48, no. 2, 2010.

Chakrabarti, Ranjan, 'Tiger and the Raj: Ordering the Maneater of the Sunderbans. 1880–1947', in *Space and Power in History: Images, Ideologies, Myths, and Moralities*, Kolkata: Penman, 2001.

Coetzee, J.M., *The Lives of Animals*, Princeton: Princeton University Press, 1999.

Crosby, Alfred W., *Ecological Imperialism: The Biological Expansion of Europe, 900–1900*, New York: Cambridge University Press, 1986.

———, *The Columbian Exchange: Biological and Cultural Consequences of 1492*, Connecticut: Greenwood Publishing Group, 1972.

Damasio, Antonio, *The Strange Order of Things: Life, Feeling, and the Making of Cultures*, New York: Pantheon Books, 2018.

Danahay, Martin A., 'Nature Red in Hoof and Paw: Domestic Animals and Violence in Victorian Art', in *Victorian Animal Dreams: Representations of Animals in Victorian Literature and Culture*, ed. Martin A. Danahay and Deborah Denenholz Morse, Surrey, England and Burlington, USA: Ashgate, 2007.

Deckha, Maneesha, 'Welfarist and Imperial: The Contributions of Anticruelty Laws to Civilizational Discourse', *American Quarterly*, vol. 65, no. 3, 2013.

DeGrazia, David, *Animal Rights: A Very Short Introduction*, Oxford: Oxford University Press, 2002.

Derrida, Jacque, *The Animal Therefore I Am*, tr. David Wills, New York: Fordham University Press, 2008.

———, *The Beast and the Sovereign*, vol. 1, tr. Geoffrey

Bennington, Chicago: University of Chicago Press, 2009.

Despret, Vinciane, 'From Secret Agents to Interagency', in *History and Theory*, vol. 52, no. 4, 2013.

Dolgert, Stefan, 'Species of Disability: Response to Arneil', *Political Theory*, vol. 38, no. 6, 2010.

Doniger, Wendy, *The Hindus: An Alternative History*, New York: Viking Press, 2009; repr., New Delhi: Speaking Tiger, 2015.

Fagan, Brian, *The Intimate Bond: How Animals Shaped Human History*, New York and London: Bloomsbury, 2015.

Fellenz, Marc R., *The Moral Menagerie: Philosophy and Animal Rights*, Chicago: University of Illinois Press, 2007.

Timothy Findley, *Not Wanted on the Voyage*, Toronto: HarperCollins, 1984.

Foltz, Richard C., *Animals in Islamic Tradition and Muslim Cultures*, Oxford: Oneworld Publications, 2007.

Francione, Gary L., *Animals as Persons: Essays on the Abolition of Animal Exploitation*, New York: Columbia University Press, 2008.

Fudge, Erica, *Animal*, London: Reaktion Books, 2002.

———, 'Milking Other Men's Beasts', *History and Theory*, vol. 52, no. 4, 2013.

Ghosh, Amitav, *The Hungry Tide*, London: HarperCollins, 2004.

Govindrajan, Radhika, *Animal Intimacies: Beastly Love in the Himalayas*, New Delhi: Viking, 2019.

Gross, Aaron and Anne Vallely, eds., *Animals and the Human Imagination: A Compilation to Animal Studies*, New York: Columbia University Press, 2012.

Gunderson, Ryan, 'The First-generation Frankfurt School on the Animal Question: Foundations for a Normative Sociological Animal Studies', *Sociological Perspectives*, vol. 57, no. 3, 2014.

Harari, Yuval Noah, *Sapiens: A Brief History of Humankind*, UK: Penguin Random House, 2011.

Haraway, Donna J., *Primate Visions*, New York: Routledge, 1989.

——, *When Species Meet*, Minneapolis: University of Minnesota Press, 2008.

Heller, Agnes, *The Theory of Need in Marx*, London: Allison and Busby, 1976.

Herzog, Harold A., 'Biology, Culture, and Origins of Pet-Keeping', in *Animal Behaviour and Cognition*, New York: Sciknow Publications, 2014.

Heymans, Peter, *Animality in British Romanticism: The Aesthetics of Species*, New York and London: Routledge, 2012.

Hills, Alison, *Do Animals have Rights?*, UK: Icon Books, 2005.

Hoquet, Thierry, 'Animal Individuals: A Plea for a Nominalistic Turn in Animal Studies', *History and Theory*, vol. 52, no. 4, 2013.

Horkheimer, Max, *Dawn and Decline: Notes, 1926–1931 and 1950–1969*, New York: Seabury Press, 1978.

—— and Theodor W. Adorno, *Dialectic of Enlightenment: Philosophical Fragments*, 1947; tr. in English, California: Stanford University Press, 2002.

Huggan, Graham and Helen Tiffin, *Postcolonial Ecocriticism: Literature, Animals, Environment*, London: Routledge, 2010.

Hussain, Shafqat, 'Sport-hunting, Fairness and Colonial Identity: Collaboration and Subversion in the Northwestern Frontier Region of the British Empire', *Conservation and Society*, vol. 8, no. 2, 2010.

——, 'Forms of Predation: Tiger and Markhor Hunting in Colonial Governance', *Modern Asian Studies*, vol. 46, no. 5, 2012.

Ingold, Tim, *Perception of The Environment: Essays on*

Livelihood, Dwelling and Skill, London: Routledge, 2011.

Jalais, Annu, *Forest of Tigers: People, Politics and Environment in the Sundarbans*, London: Routledge, 2009.

Jones, Susan D., *Valuing Animals: Veterenians and Their Patients in Modern America*, Baltimore: The Johns Hopkins University Press, 2002.

Kalof, Linda, *Looking at Animals in Human History*, London: Reaktion Books, 2007.

Karlekar, Hiranmay, *Savage Humans and Stray Dogs: A Study in Aggression*, New Delhi: Sage, 2008.

Kate, Katherine, *A Cultural History of Animals in the Age of Empire*, New York: Berg, 2007.

Kevany, Sophie Kevany, 'Millions of Farm Animals to be Culled by Suffocation', *The Guardian*, 19 May 2020, see https://www.theguardian.com/environment/2020/may/19/millions-of-us-farm-animals-to-be-culled-by-suffocation-drowning-and-shooting-coronavirus, accessed 16 February 2023.

Latour, Bruno, *Reassembling the Social: An Introduction to Actor-Network Theory*, Oxford: Oxford University Press, 2005.

Leighton, Mary Elizabeth and Lisa Surridge, 'The Empire Bites Back: The Racialized Crocodile of the Nineteenth Century', in *Victorian Animal Dreams: Representations of Animals in Victorian Literature and Culture*, ed. Martin A. Danahay and Deborah Denenholz Morse, Surrey, England and Burlington, USA: Ashgate, 2007.

Lundblad, Michael, *Animalities: Literary and Cultural Studies beyond the Human*, Edinburgh: Edinburgh University Press, 2018.

Mackenzie, John M., *The Empire of Nature: Hunting, Conservation and British Imperialism*, Manchester: Manchester University Press, 1988.

Magnum, Teresa, 'Animal Angst: Victorians Memorialize

their Pet', in *Victorian Animal Dreams: Representations of Animals in Victorian Literature and Culture*, ed. Deborah Denenholz Morse and Martin A. Danhay, Surrey, England and Burlington, USA: Ashgate, 2007.

Martel, Yann, *Life of Pi* Toronto: Random House, 2001.

Massumi, Brian, *What Animals Teach Us about Politics*, Durham NC: Duke University Press, 2014.

McFarland, Sarah E., 'The "Animal" is a Verb: Liberating the Subject of Animal Studies', *Journal of Advanced Composition*, vol. 30, nos. 3–4, 2010.

McLaughlin, Ryan P., 'Non-violence and Non-humans: Foundations for Animal Welfare in the Thought of Mohandas Gandhi and Albert Schweitzer', *The Journal of Religious Ethics*, vol. 40, no. 4, 2012.

McNeill, J.R., *Mosquito Empires: Ecology and War in the Greater Caribbean, 1620–1914*, New York: Cambridge University Press, 2010.

McNeill, William H., *Plagues and Peoples*, New York: Anchor Books, 1976.

Melandri, Francesca, 'Letter to the French from the Future', *Liberation*, 28 March 2020.

Morse, Deborah Denenholz and Martin A. Danhay, eds., *Victorian Animal Dreams: Representations of Animals in Victorian Literature and Culture*, Surrey, England and Burlington, USA: Ashgate, 2007.

Mullin, Molly H., 'Mirrors and Windows: Sociocultural Studies of Human-animal Relationships', *Annual Review of Anthropology*, vol. 28, 1999.

Nappi, Carla, 'On Yeti and Being Just: Carving the Borders of Humanity in Early Modern China', in *Animals and Human Imagination: A Companion to Animal Studies*, ed. Aaron Gross and Anne Vallely, New York: Columbia University Press, 2012.

Nelson, Lance, 'Cows, Elephants, Dogs and Other Lesser Embodiments of Atman: Reflections on Hindu Attitudes Toward Nonhuman Animals', in *A*

Communion of Subjects: Animals in Religion, Science and Ethics, ed. Paul Wadu and Kimberley Patton, New York: Columbia University Press, 2006.

Nelson, R., *Heart and Blood: Living with Deer in America*, New York: Knopf, 1997.

Nussbaum, Martha, *Frontiers of Justice: Disability, Nationality, Species Membership*, Cambridge, MA: Harvard University Press, 2007.

Oyewumi, O., *The Invention of Women: Making an African Sense of Western Gender Discourses*, Minneapolis: University of Minnesota Press, 1997.

Pandey, Gyan, 'Rallying Around the Cow: Sectarian Strife in the Bhojpuri Region, c. 1888–1917', in *Subaltern Studies 2*, New Delhi: Oxford University Press, 1983.

Pandian, Anand, 'Pastoral Power in the Postcolony: On the Biopolitics of the Criminal Animal in South India', *Cultural Anthropology*, vol. 23, no. 1, 2008.

Pearson, Chris, 'Dogs, History, and Agency' *History and Theory*, vol. 52, no. 4, 2013.

Peterson, Dale, *Eating Apes*, Berkeley and Los Angeles: University of California Press, 2003.

Premchand, *Stories on Animals*, ed. M. Asauddin, New Delhi: Viking, 2018.

Quammen, David, *Monster of God: The Man Eating Predator in the Jungles of History and the Mind*, revd. edn., New York: W.W. Norton & Company, 2004.

Rangarajan, Mahesh, *India's Wildlife History: An Introduction*, Ranikhet: Permanent Black, 2001.

Regan, Tom, *The Case for Animal Rights*, University of California Press, 1983.

Ritvo, Harriet, *The Animal Estate: The English and Other Creatures in Victorian England*, Cambridge, MA: Harvard University Press, 1989.

Samanta, Samiparna, *Meat, Mercy, Morality: Animals and Humanitarianism in Colonial Bengal, 1850–1920*, Delhi: Oxford University Press, 2021.

Satya, Laxman D., *Ecology, Colonialism and Cattle: Central India in the Nineteenth Century*, New Delhi: Oxford University Press, 2004.

Self, Will, *Great Apes*, London: Bloomsbury, 1997.

Shaw, David Gary, 'The Torturer's Horse: Agency and Animals in History', *History and Theory*, vol. 52, no. 4, 2013.

Singer, Peter, *Animal Liberation*, New York: Avon Books, 1975.

Sinha Roy, Mallarika, 'Inside/out: Women's Movement and Women in Movements', in *Women Speak Nation: Gender, Culture and Politics*, ed. Panchali Ray, Oxon and New York: Routledge, 2020.

Sinha, Suvadip and Amit R. Baishya, eds., *Postcolonial Animalities*, New York and London: Routledge, 2020.

Sinha, Suvadip, 'Pariah Dogs: Precarious Cohabiation', in *Postcolonial Animalities*, ed. Suvadip Sinha and Amit R. Baishya, New York and London: Routledge, 2020.

Sliwinski, Sharon, 'The Gaze Called Animal: Notes for a Study on Thinking', in *Selected Works of Sharon Sliwinski*, Canada: Western University, 2011.

Smail, Daniel Lord, *On Deep History and the Brain*, Berkeley: University of California Press, 2010.

———— and Andrew Shryock, eds., *Deep History: The Architecture of Past and Present*, Berkeley and London: University of California Press, 2011.

Smith, Brian K., 'Classifying Animals and Humans in Ancient India', *Man*, vol. 26, no. 3, 1991.

Smuts, Barbara B., 'Between Species: Science and Subjectivity', *Configurations*, vol. 14, nos. 1–2, 2006.

Steel, Karl, *How to Make a Human: Animals and Violence in Middle Ages*, Columbus: Ohio State University Press, 2011.

Stewart, Sandra, *Riding High: Horses, Humans and History in South Africa*, Johannesburg: Wits University Press, 2010.

Superle, Michelle, 'Animal Heroes and Transforming Substances: Canine Characters in Contemporary Children's Literature', *Animals and the Human Imagination: A Compilation to Animal Studies*, ed. Aaron Gross and Anne Vallely, New York: Columbia University Press, 2012.

Thomas, Keith, *Man and the Natural World: Changing Attitudes in England, 1500–1800*, UK: Allen Lane, 1983.

Trautmann, Thomas R., Gillian Feeley-Harnik, and John C. Mitani, 'Deep Kinship', in *Deep History: The Architecture of Past and Present*, ed. Daniel Lord Smail and Andrew Shryock, Berkeley and London: University of California Press, 2011.

Vint, Sherryl, 'Animal Studies in the Era of Biopower', *Science Fiction Studies*, vol. 37, no. 3, 2010.

Walker, Brett, 'Animals and the Intimacy of History', *History and Theory*, vol. 52, no. 4, 2013.

Wolfe, Cary, '"Human, All too Human": Animal Studies and Humanities', *Publication of the Modern Language Association*, vol. 124, no. 2, 2009.

Wolfe, Cary, *What is Posthumanism?*, Minneapolis: University of Minnesota Press, 2010.

Wadu, Paul and Kimberley Patton, eds., *A Communion of Subjects: Animals in Religion, Science and Ethics*, New York: Columbia University Press, 2006.

Unpublished Dissertations

Chatterjee, Nilanjan, 'Evolution of History Curriculum and Textbooks in Bangladesh, 1947–1990', unpublished MPhil thesis, Jadavpur University, 2020.

Samanta, Samiparna, 'Cruelty Contested: The British, Bengalis, and Animals in Colonial Bengal, 1850–1920', PhD thesis, 2012.

Index